AF254679

The
Cycle Of
Life

UNDER THE SUN

The Cycle Of Life

UNDER THE SUN

G. Oliver Barnes

The Cycle of Life Under the Sun by G. Oliver Barnes

Copyright © 2017 G. Oliver Barnes
All rights reserved. No part of this book may be reproduced
without permission from the publisher, except by a reviewer who
may quote brief passages in a review. Nor may any part of this book
be reproduced, stored in a retrieval system, or copied by mechanical,
photocopying, recording, or other means, without permission from
the publisher.

Scripture quotations are from the King James Version of the Bible
unless otherwise stated.

Library of Congress Cataloging-in-Publication Data has been applied for.
ISBN: 978-1-6-4007-781-2

Printed in the United States of America

INTRODUCTION

Here's a question for you: What lies at the center of your character when you are faced with life's ups and downs? When you face hard knocks, or the chips are down, do you give up or are you coming back for a fighting chance? We all know that life is cyclical and unpredictable. It can be filled with doubt, difficult obstacles, and regrets. No matter if you are a regular Joe or a stately royal, you will face challenges, difficulties, and adversities. The Proper response is key. Your outward response is directly related to your inward nature. But by putting each experience in perspective while following the leading of God can mean the difference between failure and success. What will you do when faced with difficulties in life? First, recognize that we are not in control of our circumstances; however, we are in control of our reaction toward each of the obstacles that come our way.

Then, realize that as you overcome the trials of life, you can turn from despair to hope. Finally, as you read this book remember that you have already overcome several challenges up to this point. Of course, there will be more trials ahead. The choices we have when faced with trials are fear, flight or fight. This book provides a look at how both big and small notable people have prevailed through their trials and is a valuable resource on how to diligently seek the Lord to conquer one test at a time.

ACKNOWLEDGEMENTS

This book is dedicated with love and affection to my dear wife Sonia who is paramount in encouraging my efforts and dreams unfailingly.
I am also thankful for my children Nicole, Kenya, Jonathan and their families for supporting me throughout this season of change in my life. My heartfelt thanks to Sis. Enid McKoy who was influential in inspiring me to trust my instincts, fear no foe and challenge myself to succeed in many areas.

Lastly, I offer my sincerest gratitude to Sis. Donna Baker and Sis. Sharon McKoy-Thompson for their efforts in typing, editing proofreading, and cheering me on in the timely pursuit of my book deadline.

Cover Design & Layout by D'edge Media, LLC / dedgemedia.com

CONTENTS

Chapter 1

■

The Cycle of Life Under the Sun

"Vanity of vanities lamented Solomon; all is vanity"! Solomon, the king, used the word vanity thirty-eight times in Ecclesiastes as he wrote about life under the sun. The word vanity means emptiness, futility, vapor, that which vanishes quickly and leaves nothing behind.

From the human point of view ("under the sun"), life does appear futile, and it is very easy for us to become pessimistic. The Jewish writer Sholem Aleichem once described life as a blister on top of a tumor, and boil on top of that. The American poet Carl Sandburg compared life to an onion; you peel it off one layer at a time, and sometimes you weep.

The British playwright George Bernard Shaw said that life was "a series of inspired lives." What a great relief to turn from these pessimistic views and hear Jesus Christ say, "I come that they may have life and that they might have it more abundantly" (John 10:10). In Paul's grand declaration, he said, "Therefore, my beloved brethren, be steadfast, unmovable, always abounding in the work of the Lord, knowing that your labor is not in vain in the Lord (1 Corinthians 15:58).

"Everything an Indian does is in a circle," said Black Elk, the Sioux religious leader. Even the seasons form a great circle in their changing and always come back again to where they were. The life of a man is a circle from childhood to childhood. For centuries, wise men and women in different nations and cultures have pondered the mysteries of the circles of human life. If life is only a part of a great cycle over which we have no control, the great question is, is the life worth living?

Solomon pondered these questions as he looked at the cycle of life "under the sun." The scientist tells us that the world is a closed system and nothing has changed. The historian says that life is a closed book and nothing is new. The philosopher tells us that life is a deep problem and nothing is understood.

Napoleon stated, "There is but one step from the sublime to the ridiculous." King Solomon examined everything from the sublime to the ridiculous. In the vast laboratory of life, he experimented with one thing after another, always applying the wisdom that God had given him. Solomon recorded three stages in his experiments as he searched for a satisfying meaning to life. He tested life (Ecclesiastes 2:1-11). The king had the means and the authority to do whatsoever his heart desired. He decided to check his own heart to see how he would respond to two common experiences of life: Enjoyment and Employment. Solomon discovered four factors that must be considered before you can say that life is monotonous and meaningless. "Few are born bold." Even Napoleon had to cultivate the habit on the battlefield where he knew it was a matter of life and death. In social settings, he was awkward and timid, but he overcame this and practiced boldness in every part of life because he saw its tremendous power; that it could enlarge a man (even one who, like Napoleon, was in fact conspicuously small).

When Solomon first examined life "under the sun" his viewpoint was detached and philosophical (Ecclesiastes 1:4-11). His conclusion was that life was meaningless and monotonous. But when he examined the question again, he went to where people lived and discovered that life was not that simple. As the king observed real people in real situations, the king had to deal with some unpleasant facts such as life and death, time and eternity, and the final judgment. The king witnessed three tragedies: (1) oppression and exploitation in the halls of justice (2) pain and sorrow in the lives of innocent people and (3) unconcern on the part of those who could have brought comfort. So, devastated was Solomon by what he saw that he decided it was better to be dead than to be alive and oppressed. In fact, one was better off if never having been born at all.

Disgusted with what he saw in the "halls of justice," the king went down to the marketplace to watch the many laborers at work.

Some Rain Must Fall

"Into each life, some rain must fall," wrote Henry Wordsworth Longfellow. He gives us the gift of life and allows us to choose the way we will use our limited time on Earth (Brainy Quote).

Great Sufferings of Paul

Are they Hebrews? So am I. Are they Israelites? So am I. Are they the seed of Abraham? So am I. Are they ministers of Christ? (I speak as a fool) I am more; in labors, more abundant,in stripes above measure, in prisons more frequent, in deaths oft. Of the Jews, five times received I forty stripes save one. Thrice was I was beaten with rods, once was I stoned, thrice I suffered shipwreck, a night and a day I have been in the deep. In journeying's often, in perils of waters, in perils of robbers, in perils by mine own countrymen, in perils by the heathen, in perils in the city, in perils in the wilderness, in perils in the sea, in perils among false brethren; In weariness and painfulness, in watchings, often, in hunger and thirst, in feastings often, in cold and nakedness (2 Corinthians 11:22-27).

Paul endured afflictions, pressure, strain and tensions that came both from within and without. Things often press in upon a man, weigh upon and burden down his heart. Sometimes the pressure is so heavy and tight that a man feels like he is going to explode or be crushed. Paul endured "necessities," inescapable hardship, difficulties, privation, and pain of life. Paul must have had incredible endurance, for he sang as he suffered (Acts 16:25).

There are only three possible outlooks a person can imagine when it comes to the trials of life. If our trials are the products of "fate" or "chance," then our only response is to give up. (1) Nobody can control fate or chance. (2) If we must control everything ourselves, then the situation is equally hopeless.

(3) But if God is in control, and we trust Him, then we can, and will overcome circumstances with His help. God encourages us in all our tribulations by teaching us from His word that it is he who permits trials to come. He is in control of tests. We are under great pressure, far beyond our ability to endure, so that we despair even of life. Paul was weighed down like a beast of burden with a load too heavy to bear, but God knew just how much Paul could take. God kept the situation in control. We do not know specifically what the trouble was, but it was significant enough to make him think he was going to die. Whether it was perils from his may enemies (see Acts 19:21; 1 Corinthians 15:30-32). Serious illness or special satanic attack, we do not know; but we do know that God controlled the circumstances and protected His servant. You see, when God puts His children into the furnace, He keeps His hand on the thermostat and His eyes on the thermometer.

Three ways prepare us for life's trials. One is the Spartan way that says, "I have strength within me to do it, I am the captain of my soul. With the courage and will that is mine, I will be the master when the struggle comes." Another way is in the spirit of Socrates, who affirmed that we have the mind, reason, and judgment to evaluate and help ourselves to cope with the enigmas and struggles of life. The Christian way is the third approach. It doesn't exclude the first two, but it adds- "You don't begin with yourself, your will, or your reason. You start with God, who is the beginning and the end. When your strength grows weak, and your reason fails, your faith in the creator gives you the power to overcome all things. (L. R. Dietzen).

The God who raises the dead is sufficient for any difficulty of life. He is able, but we must be available. Paul did not deny the way he felt, nor does God want us to deny our emotions. We are troubled on every side; without were fightings, within were fears" (2 Corinthians 7:5).

The phrase "sentence of death" in 2 Corinthians 1:9 could refer to an official verdict, perhaps an order of Paul's arrest and execution. Keep in mind that the unbelieving Jews hounded Paul's trial and wanted to eliminate him (Acts 20:19).

"Perils by own countrymen" must not be overlooked in the list of dangers (2 Corinthians 11:26). As children of the highest God, let us accept this fact that God does not always deliver us immediately, nor in the same way. James was beheaded, yet Peter was delivered from prison (Acts 12). Both were delivered but in different ways. Sometimes God delivers us from our trials, and at other times he delivers us in our trials. By so doing, He is glorified through our trials.

The subject of human suffering is not easy to understand, for there are mysteries to the working of God that we will never grasp until we get to heaven. Whatever God has allowed us to go through is to impact another person's future. You see, "The burden of suffering seems a tombstone hung about our necks, while in reality, it is only the weight which is necessary to keep down the diver while he is hunting for pearls" (Richter).

Remember that God can handle your trials and make them work out for your good and His glory. In his book, Profiles in Courage, John F. Kennedy wrote, "Great crises produce great men and great deeds of courage." While it is true that crises help to make a person, it is also true that a crisis helps to reveal what makes up a person. Pilate faced a great crisis, but his handling of it did not give him courage nor greatness. Therefore, how we handle the difficulties of life will depend largely upon what kind of character we have. For what life, does to us depends on what life finds in us.

Having Done All To Stand

What kept Paul from failing? Other people facing these same crises would have collapsed! Paul not only triumphed over the circumstances but out of them produce a great letter that even today is helping God's people experience victory.

"Victory at all cost, victory despite all terrors. Victory however long and hard the road may be; for without victory there is no survival." (Winston Churchill).

The Adversities of Life (Job 1: 6-19)

In one day, Job was stripped of his wealth. One after another, four frightened messengers came with their report that 500 yokes of oxen, 500 donkeys, and 3,000 camels were stolen in enemy raids; lightning struck 7,000 sheep and killed, and a windstorm killed all 10 of his children. King Solomon was right, "Moreover, no man knows when his hour will come: as fish is caught in a cruel net, or birds are taken in a snare, so men are trapped by evil times that fall unexpectedly upon them" (Ecclesiastics 9:12 NIV).

Your life is like a book. The title page is your name; the preface your introduction to the world. The pages are a daily record of your efforts, trial, pleasures, discouragements, and achievements. Day by day your thoughts and acts are being inscribed in your book of life. Hours by hours the record is being made that must stand for all time. Let it then be said for your book that it is a record of noble purpose, generous service, and work well done. (Glenville Kleiser).

The hosts of heaven and hell watched to see how Job would respond to the loss of his wealth and his children. He expressed his grief in a manner normal for that day, for God expects us to be human. After all, even Jesus wept (John 11:35). But Job worshiped God and uttered a profound statement of faith (Job 1:21). First, he looked back to his birth: "Naked came I out of my mother's womb." Everything Job owned was given to him by God, and the same God who gave it had the right to take it away.

Job only acknowledged that he was a steward. Then he looked ahead to his death: "And naked shall I return." The Apostle Paul wrote, "For we brought nothing into this world, and it is certain that we can carry nothing out" (I Timothy 6:7). Instead of cursing God, as Satan said Job would do, Job blessed the Lord! You see anybody can say, "The Lord gave" or "The Lord hath taken away," but it takes real vigilant courage and faith to say amid the sorrow and suffering, "Blessed be the name of the Lord." In all this Job sinned not, nor charged God with folly (Job 1:22).

A Noble Determination

What does he determine first? Never to swerve from rectitude. Till I die, I will not remove mine integrity from me. My righteousness I hold fast and will not let it go. Whatever has happened to me I will not play the fool; I will not be insincere. I will be real and ever faithful to my conscience. "My righteousness" I will hold fast. I could not ascertain the prosperity that God has blessed me with, it is gone; nor my children, they have been taken from me; nor my health, it has departed; nor my friends, for they have failed me; nor my reputation, slander has stolen it away; but my righteousness I hold fast. No one can rob me of my integrity nor destroy the consciousness that I am sincere to have it and to hold it. This is truly noble to hold it as a drowning person holds a rope thrown out for his/her rescue, firmly amidst the furious winds and dashing billows.

Thank God! We can hold it if we have it; no power in the universe can take it away without our consent.

A striking example of what a determined will can do is seen in the career of Abraham Lincoln. As a boy, he was destitute and had none of the advantages of education that the youth of today enjoy. At one time, he learned that one of his neighbors had an arithmetic book. He borrowed the book, and in the evenings after a hard day's work, he laid upon the log cabin floor and by the light of the hearth he copied the essential parts of the book. (H.F. Kletzing).

In times of severe testing, our first question must not be "How can I get out of this?" but "What can I get out of this?" Job's wife thought she had the problem solved, but if Job had followed her counsel, it would have only made things worse. The two things Job would not give up were his faith in God and his integrity, and that's what his wife wanted him to do. Therefore, when life is difficult, it is easy to give up, but giving up is the worst thing we can do. A professor of history said, "If Columbus had turned back, nobody would have blamed him, but nobody would have remembered him either." If you want your life to be memorable, sometimes you have to be miserable. In the end, Job's wife was reconciled to her husband and the Lord. God gave her another family. (Job 42:13).

I will allude to this fact that Job's strongest image is that of the tree. (Job 14:7-9). Cut it down, and its stump remains, but there is always a possibility that the tree will sprout again. The tree has hope, but the man has no hope. When he dies, he leaves no stump behind. Dead hope fades away because it is rooted in the great god of this world. The assurance of resurrection and life in glory with Christ is a strong motivation for us to keep going even when the going is tough. Many times, we have used the phrase "Been there, done that." At times God permits his children to experience darkness on a dead-end street where they don't know which way to turn. "Never doubt in the darkness what God has taught you in the light." In fact, what God teaches us in the light will become even more meaningful in the darkness (Dr. Bob Jones Sr.).

"Oh, the unspeakable benediction of the treasures of darkness!" wrote Oswald Chambers. "It's not the days of sunlight and splendor and liberty and light that leave their lasting and indelible effect on the soul, but those nights of the spirit in which, shadowed by God's hand, hidden in the dark chest of some rock in a weary land, He lets the splendors of the outskirts of himself pass before our gaze".

This is a reminder that we should begin to view life in a balanced way. Yes, God permits us to experience difficulties and sorrows, but He also sends victories, peace, and joy. Shall we not receive good at the hand of God, and shall we not receive evil? (Job 2:10).

Chapter 2

Overcoming Adversity with Outside Entities

Experiencing difficulties may come suddenly and unexpectedly, but we must maintain the standard Christ has set, endure and overcome thus giving glory to our great God. In 2006 after much research and prayer, Faith Tabernacle purchased property in Broward County, Florida. The property had once been a temple with private adjunct school. The investment seemed appropriate, and we were confident that along with our faithful tithes, our charter school would bring additional income for the church. We filed the necessary paperwork required by the city and the school board. However, each attempt to comply with the city's codes were met with resistance and rejection. To preserve the school, we moved the students to different locations while the school was being brought up to code. Unfortunately, each time the school was inspected our efforts were thwarted, which ultimately caused its doors to be closed. Meeting and communicating with city officials was a futile and humbling experience. I realized that despite all our efforts, it was inevitable that we needed to move our church to another location. God had remained ever faithful in this three-year challenge.

Woe unto them that decree unrighteousness decrees and that write grievousness laws which they have prescribed (Isaiah 10:1). Political rulers and governors of the people that made unrighteous laws which were not agreeable to the legislation of God, nor righteousness; and were injurious to the person and properties of men. Which were calculated for the oppression of good men, especially the poor; and for the protection of wicked men who made no conscience of spoiling them. They write grievousness which they have prescribed, laws grievous and intolerable beings made by them.

They wrote them or ordered them to be written, to be engrossed and obliged the people to be subjected to them. This same understood of the Scribes and Judges, who sat in courts and wrote out the decrees and sentences made by them, but it rather intends the same persons as before and not ecclesiastical but political governors are meant. Such as lived before the Babylonian captivity or otherwise the whole applies to the Scribes and Pharisee, to the miasmic doctor, the authors of the unwritten laws, the fathers of traditions, whose decisions and decrees were unrighteous and injurious and contrary to the commands of God. Heavy burdens and grievous to the bone, and very oppressive of the poor, the fatherless and the widow, for which Christ reproves them (Matthew Henry's Concise Commentary).

In Isaiah 10:1-4, these verses are to be joined with the previous chapter. Woe to the superior powers that devise and decree unrighteous decree and woe to the inferior officers that draw them up, and enter them on record! But what will sinners do? Whither will they flee unrighteous legislation? (William O. Einwechter)

This text for Isaiah is part of the Oracle or judgment against the Northern Kingdom of Israel (Isaiah 9:8-10:4). Four specific sins are singled out for the reproof by the prophets:

National pride and arrogance.
• Corrupt leaders who have led people astray.
• Civil strife and
• Cruelty and civil magistrates who oppress the people through unrighteous legislation.

The word of the Lord to the officers of Israel begins with a declaration of "woe." This word is an interjection that expresses dissatisfaction or pain. It is sometimes used as an exclamation, but often in the prophetic literature, it serves to introduce warning of impending judgment. The oracle of woe expresses God's extreme dissatisfaction with the conduct of those being addressed and announces His intention to punish them for their sins. Thus, the magistrates of Israel, the local government, and the city are put on notice that their conduct in office has excited the wrath of God.

What is it that they have done? First, they abused the power of their office by writing laws that bring hardship, trouble, and vexation to God's people. The text stated that they "decree unrighteous decrees." The verb decree refers to the action of enacting civil laws and statues. It comes from a root that means to cut, chisel or inscribe and it reflects the practices of ancient rulers of having the legislation of the land written on a stone (a standing stone or vertical slab). In Psalm 94:20, the government of wicked rulers is called a throne of iniquity because such an administration framed mischief by law. In Isaiah 10:1, Isaiah and the psalmist are speaking of the same kinds of rulers; men who abuse their powers by enacting laws that bring grief and misery to the people! Neither state, local government nor city should use their office to plunder the people they govern. This could be a great and terrible warning to those who have set themselves up to terrorize the people of God. "It is a fearful thing to fall into the hands of the living God" (Hebrew 10:31).

For God, shall bring every work into judgment, with every secret thing, whether it is good or whether it is evil. Because to every purpose, there is a time and judgment; therefore, the misery of man is great upon him. All this I have seen and applied my heart unto every work that is done under the sun. There is a time wherein one man ruled over another to his hurt. And so I saw the wicked buried who has come and gone from the place of the holy, and they were forgotten in the city where they have so done, this is also vanity. Therefore, because sentence against an evil work is not executed speedily, therefore the heart of the sons of men is fully set in them to do evil (Proverbs 28:5; Ecclesiastes 8:6, 9, 10-11).

As a pastor, I have traveled the road of hard knocks. There are folks within and without the church who have asked and are still asking, "How did you pull through this?" They saw me laugh and weep many times, even ending up in the hospital to have one of my toes amputated. Even so, I will always have a word for the concerned folks.

"What we laugh at and what we weep over indicates our values of life under the sun." Whenever you enter the presence of joy, you make yourself a candidate of sorrow. Many things in life that bring joy can also bring sorrow.

I saw Wicked (rulers) buried, who came into the world and went from the Holy Place (the seat of authority and justice, see Deuteronomy 19:17), Chronicles 19:6) then were forgotten in the city where they had so ruled to the hurt of their subjects: This, their death and oblivion - shews their lot to be vanity. (Barnes Notes on the Bible).

The authority to legislate is from God, who is the King and Supreme Law-Giver for all men. Therefore, magistrates must not rule autonomously but in strict submission to the laws of God as they establish these laws that will concern those under their jurisdiction. There is a "Woe" that is pronounced upon any magistrate or city council who restrain the office of civil rulers. When men who hold the office in any place or time corrupt it, God is extremely dissatisfied with them and they fall under His curse. The authority to legislate and decide cases in the civil sphere is from God and must not be abused. The magistrate and city council are responsible for defending and protecting the God-given rights of its citizens. The overriding concern of magistrates and city councils is justice for all.

This is their calling! They should not be partial, socialistic and humanistic. You see, laws that are contrary to God's law wreak havoc and misery on society. God's law is the perfect law of liberty. When His law is the basis of society's governance, there will be freedom, prosperity, and justice. Laws that strip the weak and needy of their rights is especially offensive to God. Leaders in authority, who abuse their influence and power through unrighteous legislation, face judgment both in this life and beyond the grave. Magistrates who pervert their office will not escape God's sanctions. They will suffer in this life and will have to give a full account in the next. Truly the oracle of judgment in Isaiah 9:8-10:4 describe the sins of our time; and unless we repent, our fate will be the same as the Northern Kingdom of Israel (Christian Statesman Vol. 144, no.2, April 2001).

Here is the challenge: To whom he will flee with all their pride and power to outface the judgments of God? Where will you leave your glory to find it again when the storm is over? (Isaiah 10:3). Rulers in high places have engaged themselves to do evil, kept secret, done in secrecy, especially for evil, immoral or illegal purpose: a clandestine intelligence operation.

Be Encouraged

Who shall separate us from the love of Christ? Shall tribulation or distress or persecution, or famine or nakedness of peril or sword? As it is written, for thy sake we are killed all the day long. We are accounted as sheep for the slaughter. Nay, in all these things we are more than conquerors through Him that love us. For I am persuaded that, that neither death, nor life nor angels nor principalities, nor powers, nor things present, nor things to come, nor height, nor depth, nor any other creatures shall be able to separate us from the love of God, which is in Christ Jesus our Lord (Romans 8:35-39). This is the bond of union with Christ, and the union which is made by it is exceeding near and close, it is real, perfect and indissoluble. Nothing can separate us from His love. Not affliction, which springs from His love, the fruit of it and notwithstanding that, we rest in His love. This is not taken away but is often sensibly enjoyed, during afflictions or distress. Whether of the body or mind. Straightness in the affairs and circumstances of life or straightness of minds in the exercise of grace and discharge of duty. For though we believe not, yet He abides faithful, to His covenant and promises. It is no ground of confidence to assert that we will never forsake Christ, but it is the strongest ground of assurance to be convinced that His love will never change. Shall tribulation, "None of these, nor all together, how terrible the flesh, or tokens of God's wrath or least ground for doubt of His love. From whom could such a question come better than from one who had himself for Christ's sake endured so much? See 1 Corinthians 4:10. He that hath prepared a crown and a kingdom for us will give us what we need in the way of it. Men may justify themselves, though the accusations are in full force against them if God explains that answers all. By Christ, we are thus secured. By the merits of His death, he paid our debt. Yea, rather that rises again. This is convincing evidence that divine justice was satisfied. We have such a friend in Jesus to whom all powers are given. He has always been there with us making intercession.

Then do not toss your spirit and perplex your thoughts in fruitless and endless doubting. But as you are convinced of ungodliness, believe on Him who justifies the ungodly. None can take Christ from the believer: none can take the believer from Him, and that is enough. All other hazard signifies nothing. Alas, poor sinners! Though you abound with the possessions of this world. What vain things are they! Can you say of any of them, who shall separate us? You may be removed from pleasant dwellings, and friends and estates. You may even live to see and seek your partying. At least you must part, for you must die. Then, farewell, all this world accounts most valuable. And what hast thou left, the poor soul who hast not Christ, but that which thou wouldest gladly part with, and canst not, the condemning guilt of all thy sins! But the soul that is in Christ, when other things are pulled away, cleaves to Christ and these separations pain Him not. Yea, when death comes that breaks all other unions, even that of the soul and body, it carries the believer's soul into the presence of God. (Matthew Henry's concise commentary, Jamieson- Fausset- Brown Bible Commentary).

For by Him all things were created: things in Heaven and on earth, visible and invisible, whether thrones or powers or rulers or authorities. He created all things. "Here is the clear statement that Christ is the creator and ruler over all authorities, whether they submit to Him or rebel against Him. Therefore, whatever power the evil forces possess, they are not out of ultimate control of our sovereign God. Who uses even the wicked for bringing about His perfect plan and purpose? The Savior, by His death, took dominion from every act of enemy and devil and got back what they have captured. Satan and His legions had invaded the earth and drawn humanity into captivity, subjecting them into their evil reign. But Christ, by His death, subdued the invaders and recaptured those who had been vanquished. Colossians 2:14 speaks of Jesus being nailed to the cross along with the written charges against us.

The Final Destiny of the Wicked

Every view of the world has its eschatology. It cannot help raising the question of whether, as well as what and whence? "O, my Lord": said Daniel to the angels, "What shall be the end of these things?" (Daniel 12:8).

What is the end, the final destiny of the wicked? Does he perish at death, or does he enter another state of being, and under what conditions of happiness or how does he exist there? What is the end, the final aim of the great whole, that far off divine event towards which the whole creation moves? It is vain to tell a man not to ask these questions. He will ask them, and they must ask him. He will pour over every scrap of facts or trace of law which seems to give an indication of an answer. He will try from the experience of the past, and the knowledge of the present, to deduce what the future shall be. He will peer as far as He can to the unseen, and where knowledge fails, will weave from his hopes and trusts pictures and conjectures. The Christian view of the world also has its eschatology. "The Christian view, however, is positive, where that of science is negative, ethical, where it is material, human, where it is cosmogony, ending in personal immortality where this ends in extinction and death. The eschatology of Christianity springs from its character as a teleological religion – it seeks to grasp the unity of the world through the concept of an end or aim" (James Orr).

This is probably the hardest of all the doctrines of Christianity to be received. If we ask the reason, we receive various answers: Some will tell us that this doctrine is unwelcome to many because they feel guilty, and their conscience tells them that unless they repent and turn to God this awful dome awaits them. Others believe that it is because the thought of future punishment strikes terror to people's heart and therefore this doctrine is repulsive to them. The future punishment of the wicked holds a prominent place in the teachings of the scriptures that can be no reasonable doubt. After all, it's not the sayings of hard things that pierces the conscience of the people; it's the voice of the divine love heard amid the thunder. (The Great Doctrines of the Bible; Eng. Ed., pp 256-257).

There Will Be Hope

Believers will be delivered from the great misery facing mankind of "having no hope" (Ephesians 2:12). Christians eagerly expect at least seven revealed certitudes. All of them are doubtless comprehended in "the hope of His callings. (Ephesians 1:18), the hope which is laid up for you in heaven, (Colossians 1:5). **The seven are:**

The blessed hope of the personal return of Christ (Titus 2:13).
The resurrection of the body in a glorious new form, never again subject to sickness weakness or death, Acts 23:6.
The restoration of loved ones who have fallen asleep in Christ, (I Thessalonians 4:13-18).

Fellowship with coverts and other saints, (I Thessalonians 2: 19).
Being presented spotless, (2 Peter 3:14) and faultless, (Jude 24).
Entering eternal life with all its means such as reigning with Christ, (Revelation 3:21; 22:3) and knowing who our great God is.

The receiving of an inheritance which is reserved in heaven until that moment, (1 Peter 1:3-4). This exceedingly rich array of blessings is to believers a source of joy (Romans 5:2). Of comfort in sorrow (I Thessalonians 4:18), of confident assurance (Hebrew 6: 18-19). It is an incentive to holy living. Christians are said to be saved in hope, (Romans 8:24), a hope based on the written word of God (Psalm 119:49).

Praise be to the God of glory, our Lord Jesus Christ! In His great mercy, he has given us new birth into a living hope through the resurrection of Jesus Christ from the dead (I Peter 1:3). And into an inheritance that can never perish, spoil or fade-kept in heaven for you (1 Peter 1:4). To him who overcomes, I will give the right to sit with me on my throne, just as overcame and sat down with my Father on His throne (Revelation 3:21).

"Nothing is easy in war," said Dwight Eisenhower. Wicked and evil men can and will cause God's children to be discouraged. You see, discouragement in ministry knows no bounds. It spreads across denominations, religions and all cultures. It strikes politicians and seasoned pastors no exceptions to the rule. Therefore, discouragement breaks some people. They walked away from the ministry. "For this reason, I also suffer these things; nevertheless, I am not ashamed, For I know whom I have believed and I am persuaded that he can keep what I have committed to Him until that day" (2 Timothy 1:12 NKJV).

Chapter 3

A Strength for Endurance

I t's one thing to experience God's power when you are facing giants or fighting armies, and quite something else when you are watching people tear your world apart. God was chastening David, but he knew that God's power could help him in the hour of pain as well as in the hour of conquest. He wrote in one of his exile Psalms, "Many there be which say of my soul, there is no help for him in God. But thou, O Lord art a shield for me. My glory, and the lifter up of mine head." (Psalm 3:2-3).

I cried unto the Lord with my voice, with my voice unto the Lord did I make my supplication. I poured out my complaint before him; I shewed before Him my trouble. When my spirit was overwhelmed within me, then thou knowest my path. In the way, wherein I walked have they privily laid a snare for me? David, the king, says, I looked on my right hand and beheld, but there was no man that would know me: refuge failed me: no man cared for my soul. I cried unto thee, O Lord: I said, Thou art my refuge and my portion in the land of the living. Attend unto my cry, for I brought very low: deliver me from my persecutors for they are stronger than I. Bring my soul out of prison, that I may praise thy name: the righteous shall compass me about, for thou shalt deal bountifully with me (Psalm 142: 1-7). David recognized that God's loving hand of discipline was upon him and he admitted that he deserved every blow. But he also believed that God's gracious hand of power was still at work as He forsook Saul. The Lord was still working out His perfect will, and never did David rise to greater heights of faith and submission than when he was forced to leave Jerusalem and hide in the wilderness.

Under chastening, all manner of affliction that God layeth upon His children are comprised. They are called chastening, because of the end that God aimeth at in afflicting them, which is their good. By this, we may discern an especial reason for that little good which many gains by crosses, they fail of observing this main condition. They may bear the cross because they cannot cross it off, but they do not endure it contentedly, willingly in obedience to God. Thou (You) mayest learn at this moment how to gain good by affliction, even by enduring them! Therefore, be careful to observe well these few directions:

Look to God that smiteth, and duly weigh His Supreme Sovereignty, His almighty power, His unsearchable wisdom, His free grace, His rich mercy, His great forbearance, and other like excellences.

Be circumspect over your inward disposition, to keep yourself from fretting, vexing, and perplexing the spirit.

Be watchful over your outward behavior, that thou manifest no discontent there is.

Be well informed in the manifold trials whereunto the best is subject in this world.

Take thyself an invincible courage and resolution to hold out, and still prepare thyself for more when some are passed.

In all the scripture, only one man has ever been called a man after God's own heart (Acts 13:22). Not Enoch, who walked with God and "was not" because God took him (Genesis 5:24), not Abraham, by whose name God chose to identify Himself (Exodus 3:15). Not Joseph, a man whom God granted favor (Genesis 39:21). Not Moses, who talked with God face-to-face (Numbers 12:8), nor Joshua, Samuel, Solomon, Elijah, nor even Daniel. The only man God called a man after His own heart was David, the son of Jesse.

During his lifetime, he weathered every kind of storm, imaginable, the vicissitudes of life that come to us all, the trouble others bring, but nothing was as devastating as the trouble he brought upon himself and those he loved through his irresponsible and sinful choices. David is the only king to be born in Bethlehem, the savior's birthplace. David is called "The Lord's anointed" a threefold anointing to kingship was his:

By Samuel privately (1 Samuel 16:11).

By his tribe, Judah (11 Samuel 4:2).

By all of Israel (11 Samuel 5:2)

Warren Wierbbe writes, "our values determine or evaluations. If we value comfort more than character, then trials will upset us. If we value the material and physically more than the spiritual, we will not be able to count it all joy. If we live only for the present and forget about the future, the trial will make us bitter, not better."

The Benefits of Endurance

James the Apostle once said, "Blessed is the man that endureth temptation: for when he is tried, he shall receive the crown of life, which the Lord hath promised to them that love Him." The Greeks had a race in their Olympic games that was unique. The winner was not the runner who finished first. It was the runner who finished with his torch still lit. I want to run all the way with the flame of my torch still lit for Him (J. Stowell, Fan the Flame).

We all have been challenged by the writer of the book of Hebrews. "Wherefore seeing we also are compassed about with so great a cloud of witness, let us lay aside every weight, and the sin which doth so easily beset us, and let us run with patience the race that is set before us, looking unto Jesus the author and finisher of our faith; who for the joy that was set before Him Endured the cross, despising the shame, and is set down at the right hand of the throne of God" (Hebrews 12:1-2). Be patient, therefore, brethren, unto the coming of the Lord. Behold, the husbandman waiteth for the precious fruit of the earth, and hath long patience for it, until he receives the early and latter rain (James 5:7).

Life Waiting Stages

Life is composed of waiting periods. The child must wait until he is old enough to have a bicycle, the young man until he is old enough to drive a car, the medical student must wait for his diploma, the husband for his promotion, the young couple for savings to buy a new home. The art of waiting is not learned at once (Howard Whitman).

The bee has been applying described as "busy." The bee must visit 56,000 clover heads to produce one pound of honey. Each head has 60 flower tubes. A total of 3,360,000 visits is necessary to give us that pound of honey for the breakfast table. Meanwhile, that worker bee has flown the equivalent of three times around the world. Therefore, to produce one teaspoon of honey for our toast, the little bee makes 4,200 trips to flowers. He makes about ten flights a day to the fields, each trip lasting twenty minutes on average and four hundred flowers. An average worker bee will fly as far as eight miles if he cannot find a nectar flow that is nearer. "Human life is everywhere a state in which much is to be endured and little to be enjoyed" (Samuel Johnson).

We've been encouraged by these words from the Apostle Paul, "Therefore, my beloved brethren, be ye steadfast, unmovable, always abounding in the work of the Lord, for as much as ye know that your labor is not in vain in the Lord" (1 Corinthian 15:58). Stand fast therefore in the liberty wherewith Christ hath made us free, and be not entangled again with the yoke of bondage (Galatians 5:1). Let us look at those who have gone before us – men and women who believed and hoped in God. They faced all kinds of trials and temptations, but they patiently endured; combated and conquered them all. Look at the prophets, and you will see a great example to follow in patience endurance.

As Hebrews says: "They suffered cruel mocking and scourging, yea more over of bonds and imprisonment: they were stoned, they were sawn asunder, were tempted, were slain with the sword: they wandered about in sheepskins and goatskins; being destitute, afflicted; of whom the world was not worthy, they wandered in the deserts, and in mountains, and in dens and caves of the earth" (Hebrews 11: 36-38).

The Cycle of Life Under the Sun

The prophets patiently endured all the trials and temptations of life. They stood fast, held onto their faith in God, and combated the trials and temptations every step of the way. Few people ever suffer the trials and temptations of "life under the sun" as much as Job suffered. He suffered utter bankruptcy, the loss of all his property, livestock, and employees, and then, in the severest blow of all, he lost all his children in an accident. In addition to all this, his wife chastised him because he refused to complain and curse God for destroying their lives. But note this: Job never gave in to his trials or temptations. He never forsook his faith in God. He did not understand all that was happening to him, but he refused to turn against God. He stood and patiently endured, struggling to conquer in the name of his God. Merriam-Webster Dictionary explains endurance as "the ability to do something difficult for a long time, capacity to deal with the pain of suffering that continues for a long time. The quality of remaining for a long time.

How can we combat and conquer the temptations of life? Two steps must be taken. First, be patient and endure, keep your eyes fixed upon the return of the Lord Jesus Christ. The second step is to take each circumstance and respond to it appropriately. Circumstances that throw us into a helpless situation are almost innumerable. But there is excellent news. The Lord promises to help us conquer all helpless situations. He promised to give us the strength to endure and to walk through life's trials triumphantly. Overcoming any hardship or misfortune, no matter how severe. Listen to what God's Holy Words say:

"There hath no temptation taken you but such as is common to man: But God is faithful, who will not suffer you to be tempted above that ye are able; but will with temptation also make a way of escape, that ye may be able to hear it" (1 Corinthians 10:13). "And the Lord shall deliver me from every evil work, and will preserve me unto His heavenly kingdom: to whom be glory forever, Amen" (2 Timothy 4:18).

The first and final thing you must do in this world is to last in it and not be smashed by it, and it's the same way with your work. This is at once a rule for the conduct of life and a rule for the conduct of art: to last and to work that will last (Ernest Hemingway).

Trials force you to respond. You can flee, fight or fly above them. Be sure God has a purpose in your trial and wants you to learn how to fly above it. If we keep running away, we are like children who never grow up. We don't need the wings of a dove to fly away. We need the wings of an eagle, the prophet Isaiah, says, "Those who wait on the Lord shall renew their strength, they shall mount up with wings like eagle "(Isaiah 40:31). The Eagles know how to endure, face the storm, spread its wings and allow the wind to lift it above the storm. Please take a moment to explore Psalm 57:1-11. David wrote this song when he fled from Saul into a cave. It's difficult to sing even amid the blessings of life, so how could David possibly turn this situation into a song? How could he turn a cave into a cave hall? David was a great soldier. But he also was a great singer. Despite difficulties and problems and even dangers, he was able to endure and praise the Lord.

"Sure, I am this day we are masters of our fate, that the task which has been set before us is not above our strength; that its pangs and toils are not beyond our endurance. As long as we have faith in our cause and an unconquerable will to win, victory will not be denied us." (Sir Winston Churchill, 1871-1965).

Someone has said that there are three stages of life: Childhood, Adolescence and "My, you're looking good." We can't stop aging. But no matter how old we grow, we ought to continue increasing in the Lord. "The righteous shall flourish like the palm tree; he shall grow like a cedar in Lebanon. Those who are planted in the house of the Lord shall flourish in the courts of our God. They shall still bear fruits in old age; they shall be fresh and flourishing" (Psalm 92:12-14). Palm trees stand a lot of abuse, storms, and winds. The winds that break other trees bends the palm tree, but then it comes back up. Palm trees have roots that go down deep to draw up the water in the deserted area. Palm trees survive when other trees are dying. Also, they just keep on producing fruit. Through this great endurance; the fruit doesn't diminish; it gets better and sweeter.

The path of your walk with God is lined with both trials and blessings. When the way becomes rough and challenging. He promises sure fitting to get over the obstacles.

You may be going through the furnace right now if so remember that one reason you endure such difficulties is, so you will discover that the word of God is pure, refined and trustworthy. Growth is often a painful process; it is through difficulty and distress that God enlarges us. Therefore, it is important that you waste not your trials by simply enduring them or waiting to be delivered from them. Allow trials to have their perfect work of enlarging you for a greater ministry. This is a good reminder that we should try to see life in a balanced way. You see, God permits us to experience difficulties and sorrows, but God also sends victories and joy. Shall we receive good at the hand of God, and shall we not receive evil? When we are experiencing trials, it's natural for us to long for the good old days; but our longing will not change our situation. This is the moment in our lives when we should strive to preserve the spirit of endurance.

If we focus so much on the glories and the challenges of the past that we ignore the opportunities of the present, we may end up unprepared to meet the future. We should be wise enough to know that we must face the reality of the present and not escape into the memory of the past. People who refuse to come to grips with life are in danger of losing touch with reality, and soon they lose touch with themselves.

Which Kind Are You?

A lot of Christians are like wheelbarrows - not good unless pushed. Some are like canoes-they need to be paddled. Some are like kites - if you don't keep a rein on them, they fly away. Some are like kittens - they are more contended when petted. Some are like football - you can't tell what way they will bounce next. Some are like balloons - full of wind and ready to blow up. Some are like trailers - they have to be pulled. Some are like lights - they keep going on and off. And there are those who always seek to let the Holy Spirit lead them through the spirit of endurance.

As the flame of the lamp or the spark in the dark, life is a precious but delicate thing. It doesn't take a very strong wind to blow it out. "There is but a step between me and death" (I Samuel 20:3). History tells us that Edison refused to admit defeat. He continued without sleep for two days and nights.

Finally, he managed to slip off the carbonized threads into a vacuum-sealed bulb. And he turned on the current. "The sight we so long desired to see finally met our eyes." His persistence, endurance amidst such discouraging odds has given the world the great electric light! When life is hard it's easy to give up, but giving up is the worst thing we can do. A professor of history said, "If Columbus had turned back, nobody would have blamed him, but nobody would have remembered him either." If you want to be memorable, sometimes you have to be miserable. God's words tell us, "In the end, Job's wife was reconciled to her husband and the Lord, and God gave her another family (Job 42:13).

Chapter 4

■

Walk With Dignity

And Enoch lived sixty and five years, and begat Methuselah: and Enoch walked with God after he begat Methuselah three hundred years, and begat sons and daughters. And all the days of Enoch were three hundred and sixty and five years, and Enoch walked with God, and he was not, for God took him (Genesis 5:21-22).

What an epitaph about this ancient saint! It is as clear-cut today as when first recorded here. We know nothing of Enoch but this brief history, but it tells us everything. It was not an act or some acts, but a high tone of life consistently maintained. Better to walk with God every day in calm, unbroken fellowship than to have occasional rapturous experiences, succeeded by long relapses and backslidings. The Hebrew word might be rendered, Enoch walked and continued to walk. Enoch was a Gentile. He is mentioned three times in Scripture. Apart from that, we know nothing about him. The Holy Spirit is silent about all the common facts of his life. We are aware of nothing about his boyhood, his schooling, or his occupation. We have no idea what was his physical appearance. We know his father's name and his son's name, but do not know his mother's name or his wife's name. We do not know if he was considered brilliant or backward, cautious or confident, gregarious or aloof. We do not know if he was rich or poor; famous or despised loved or feared. Out of complete obscurity, he suddenly surfaced as a candidate for the rapture and the voice of God in an apostate age. His name means "dedicated," "consecrated," "separated." He became Enoch the immortalized because he was Enoch the sanctified.

Jude picks up Enoch's story, adds to it by direct revelation and inspiration of the Holy Spirit, and moved on.

Jude uses him as a contrast to Cain, Balaam, and Korah. Those three men were the apostates of their age; Enoch was the faithful believer of his. Korah went to hell; Enoch went to heaven. Cain went his way and became a stranger and a vagabond on the earth. Enoch walked with God and became a pilgrim and a stranger on the earth but a citizen of heaven. Balaam loved gold. Enoch loved God, just as end time apostasy heralds the rapture of the church and the doom of the world. This is the ultimate in Christian experience: When Enoch walked with God, the Lord took him home! To walk with the Lord means stopping when he stops and continuing when He moves. People often say to their children, "They must crawl before they walk, and they must walk before they can run." That is not so with God's babies! They can fly before they can run and run before they can walk. This path leads to spiritual maturity. Writing to the church at Sardis, the Lord said, "Thou hast a few names even in Sardis which have not defiled their garments, and they shall walk with me in white: for they are worthy." (Revelation 3:4). It was regrettable that to this church with its magnificent reputation, the Lord said: "Thou hast a name that thou livest and art dead" (Revelation 3:1). Even in Sardis, there were believers who had not defiled their garments. They would walk with Christ in eternity as they had walked with Him on earth. No one can walk with the Lord and at the same time be far from Him. John the beloved tells us, "But if we walk in the light, as He is in the light, we have fellowship one with another and the blood of Jesus Christ his Son cleanseth us from all sin (1 John 1:7). The author of "Walk in the Light," Bernard Barton, was known as "England's Quaker Poet." Although he never rose above the position of a bank clerk, his reputation as a man of letters was recognized by many literary leaders of his day. In all, Barton had ten books of verse published, from which approximately 20 hymns came into usage. It was William Cowper, 1731-1800 who composed the beautiful hymn, "O for a Closer Walk With God."

The Christian life begins with a step of faith for salvation. Then it continues step by step towards spiritual maturity as we develop a growing closeness to God. If we sincerely desire a more intimate relationship with our Lord, we will need perseverance and often personal denial or sacrifice.

As we endeavor to walk closely with God, unscheduled events will often come into our lives. Yes, these unexpected happenings may result in great blessings than we have ever expected. Therefore, if we learn to be flexible and calmly trust God to lead us in His way, we will not only be drawn closer to Him but will be more aware or His glorious presence.

The life of William Cowper was filled with troubling events. Early in life, he began to be plagued with chronic melancholy and depression that afflicted him at various time until his death. At one time, he was in such mental torment that he even attempted to drown himself. In 1779, his outstanding talent inspired him to produce the great and famous Olney Hymns Hymnal. One of the most significant contributions of evangelical hymnology. Cowper wrote 67 of the texts in this book. This hymn test was originally titled "Walking with God," based on Genesis 5:24, "Enoch walked with God: And he was not; for God took him. Enoch's life was an embodiment of the Divine Devoted to God..

He was:
- **Intimately acquainted with God.**
- **In constant fellowship with God.**
- **Full of confidence in God.**
- **Engaged in active service for God.**

This was indeed a great career remarkable in its termination "translated." 1. Exempted from the great trial of life. He was too full of the living God to die. There was a special honor for his extraordinary holiness. An intimation of how all might have been taken out of the world had there been no sin. A prophecy of victory over death for all the good at the resurrection. Enoch was removed from the world in a unique manner. Pleasant, mysterious, final, suggestive, proving: A). That there is a future state, B). That the body and soul exist hereafter C). That the departed good dwell with God forever. (B.D. Johns).

Enoch, one of the world's great teachers.

1). It is strange that so little is said about Enoch.
2). His stay on earth was comparatively short.
3). The manifest singularity of the life he lived.

Walk with Dignity

Enoch taught the world by his life. He walked with God. This implies an abiding consciousness of the divine presence, warm fellowship, spiritual progress. He pleased God. As the loadstar seems to beam more brilliantly in the firmament the darker grow the clouds that float above it, so Enoch's life must have been a luminous power in his age of black depravity. He taught the word by his translation that death is not a necessity of human nature. There is a sphere of human existence beyond this; There is a God in the universe who approves of goodness; Mastering of sin is the way to a grand destiny. He taught the world of his preaching, the advent of the Judges, the gathering of the saints, the conviction of the sinners. The holy life which resulted from Enoch led him to please God. This pleasing God was accompanied by the testimony that he pleased Him. And so, this statement enabled him to walk with God. It is, then, above all things important to know how men are led to please God. Here, it must be observed that people never attain the state of existence which is now to be described, while they are left to the ordinary operation of their faculties and governed by the normal impulses of their passions and desires. Anyone cannot justly question that the pleasure of God in man is connected with the conformity of man in heart and life to the laws of God. One thing that must be remarked by way of caution; God is not pleased with man's holiness because there is anything or original or independent merit in it. He is satisfied with it because He contemplates in it His work; Just as He was pleased when, after the creation, he looked on it, and pronounced that it was "good." He is satisfied with it, because it sheds His luster, and reflects the beauty of His perfection. He is pleased with it, because it advances the revenue of His glory because it secures the happiness of those in whom dwells. Those who exist in a state that is pleasing to God are privileged with near and intimate communion with God. Those who live in this state also possess the consolations and support of God in all times of difficulty and of danger. Pleasing God involves sharing a special connection with the joy of God. Enoch walked alone with God in his simplicity and holy dignity. "He pleased God." And then God took him after three hundred and sixty-five earthly years had been given to him. God took him; to show to the ungodly world that he was not limited to the ordinary operations of the laws of nature. He proclaimed to the race of giants, the children of Cain, His authentication of His servant's life. He translated him.

Enoch opposed the current opinions of the day: the primary and grand distinction between the child of God and the servant of sin is, that one lives by faith and the other by sight. Enoch lived above the present world, and apart from the present people, by faith; above all, in his religion behold the man of faith' What he does is not to be seen of men, but His Father in heaven, who shall reward him openly.

Success is not distinction, but the road that you're on. Being successful means that you are working hard and walking your walk every day. You can only live your dreams by working hard towards it. That's living your dream (Marlon Wayans).

The greatest single cause of the atheism in the world today is Christians who acknowledge Jesus with their lips and walk out the door and deny Him by their lifestyle. That is what an unbelieving world simply finds unbelievable (Brennan Manning).

Be ye, therefore, followers of God, as dear children; and walk in love as Christ also hath loved us, and hath given Himself for us an offering and a sacrifice to God for a sweet-smelling savor (Ephesians 5:1-2). There must be no dark moments between us if we are going to walk with God. Amos 3:3 asks a profound question, "Can two walk together, except they are agreed?" God and man cannot walk together, except they agree. Unless we seek His glory, we cannot walk with him. Therefore, let us not presume on outward privileges, without special sanctifying grace. (Matthew Henry Concise Commentary).

Can two walk together except they agree? Unless they meet at an appointed time and place, when and where they shall set out, what road they will take, and whether they will go. Without such consultation and agreement, it cannot be thought they should walk together; and not amicably, unless united in friendship, and are of the same affliction to each other, and of the same sentiments one with another; or it is much if they do not fall out by the way.

The design of these words is to show, that without friendship there is no fellowship. Without Concord, no communion; as this is the case between man; and man; so between God and man.

Walk with Dignity

Israel could not expect that God should walk with them, and show Himself friendly, to them, when they walked contrary to him. The Israelites were so disagreeable to Him in their sentiments of religion and their worship. Their conduct and behavior were unacceptable. To enjoy a spiritual walk with God, and communion with Him, an agreement is requisite.

There is therefore now no condemnation to them which are in Christ Jesus, who walk not after the flesh, but after the Spirit (Romans 8:1).

This is the result of the complete divine provision which is made for our justification. There is no damnatory sentence against those who walk after the spirit. There is no curse hanging like a thundercloud over their heads. There is no penal consequence following them. "Who walk"- that is, who act and who live "Not after the flesh" that is, not under the influence of the things appeal to the eye and the ear of the body. - Not under the power of the feelings which these things chiefly awaken and appear to and not according to the impulses and desires of human nature in its unsanctified state. Who walk not after the flesh, but after the spirit. That is, in obedience to the dictates of the spirit, and in response to the propensities of a soul possessed, not by the world, but owned and move in all its impulses and all its resolutions by the spirit of God and the spirit of holiness.

Believers may be chastened of the Lord, but will not be condemned with the world; by their union with Christ through faith. They are secured. What is the principle of their walk: The flesh or the Spirit, the old or the new nature, corruption or grace? For which of these do we make provisions, by which are we governed? The unrenowned will is unable to keep any commandment fully.

Therefore, we are buried with Him by baptism into death, that like as Christ was raised up from the dead by the glory of the Father, even so, we also should walk in newness of life (Romans 6:4).

Thou my everlasting portion, more than friend of life to me, all along my pilgrim journey, Savior, let me walk with thee. Close to Thee, Close to Thee, all along my pilgrim journey, Savior, let me walk with thee. Not for ease or worldly pleasure, not for fame, my prayer shall be; Gladly will I toil and suffer, only let me walk with thee.

Lead me through the vale of shadows, Bear me O'er life fitful sea, Then the gate of life eternal, May I enter, Lord with Thee, Close to Thee, Close to Thee, Close to Thee, Close to Thee, Then the gate of life eternal, may I enter, Lord with Thee (Fanny Crosby).

As a people of God, we are being summoned by God to walk holy. The Apostle Paul says, "Awake thou that sleepest and arises from the dead, and Christ shall give thee light. See then that ye walk circumspectly, not as fools, but as wise (Ephesians 5: 14-15). See then that ye walk circumspectly. The Alexandrian copy on the Vulgate Latin version read, "See then, brethren." It is an exhortation to the saints at Ephesus, upon the foregoing discourse and citation, to take heed to their walk: the believer's walk is both inward and outward. His/her inward is by faith on Christ, his/her outward walk is his/her conversation among men: this walk should be seen to, and watched over; a man should see to it that he does walk, and to the way in which he walks, and how he walks circumspectly, with his eyes on him, that he walks with diligence, caution, accuracy, and exactness, to the uttermost of his strength and power; and with wisdom and prudence looking well to his going not as fools, but as wise. Such walk like fools whose eyes are not upon their ways, who walk in their ways (Gillis Exposition of the Entire Bible).

Which are crooked, and ways of darkness, and lead to the destruction; who walk after the flesh, and naked, without the garments of a holy life and conversation; and with lamps, but no oil in them and such walk as wise men, who walk accordingly to the rule of God's word, make Christ their pattern, have the Holy Spirit for their guide and walk as becomes the Gospel of Jesus Christ; inoffensively to all men, in wisdom towards them that are without, and in love to them that are within; and as pilgrims and strangers in this world, looking for a better country and so as to promote the glory of God, and the good of souls.

Folly brings joy to one who has no sense, but whoever has understanding keeps a straight course (Proverbs 15:21).

Do not walk loosely, without fixed principles of action; but make sure that your walking is not utter folly that is reproved, but easy-mindedness, want of earnest consideration in a matter so infinitely vital, so as to know what is truly best. Walk circumspectly, that ye may keep within the line of your duty. You see, religion is not an extensive plain, in which you may walk at large, and turn to ay point without passing its limits; but a strait and narrow path, in which you must pursue; one steady course without diverting to either side. Be watchful to retain a sense of virtue and rectitude. Be attentive, that you may conform to the spirit of God commands. Walk circumspectly, that you may escape the snares in your way. Your greatest security lies in watchfulness and prayer, lest you enter into temptation. If they meet you, resist them, but your first care is to avoid them. Walk circumspectly, that you may wisely comport with the aspects of providence. In the day of prosperity be joyful, and in the day of adversity consider. Be circumspect, that he may do every duty in its time and place. Walk circumspectly, that your good may not be evil spoken of, the days are evil. The Christian, while he dwells on earth, may say, "The days are evil," because he finds in himself much disorder and corruption because he is exposed to various afflictions because there are many adversaries because iniquity abounds. If we walk with our heads lifted by pride, we shall miss our footing, and slip from the path.

Chapter 5

───────■───────

Walk in the Word

Thy word have I hid in my heart, that I might not sin against thee (Psalm 119:11). For the word of God is quick, and powerful, and sharper than any two-edged sword, piercing even to the dividing asunder of soul and spirit, and of the joints and marrows, and is a discerner of the thoughts and intents of the heart. (II Corinthians 2:17)

Among the many promises that Christ has given us is this: "If ye abide in me, and my words abide in you, ye shall ask what ye will, and it shall be done unto you" (John 15:7). Christ's words dwelling in us not only gives us the authority to pray and directs us as to the petitions we should make but also gives us the incentive to prayer. When we come in the spirit of faith to the word of God, it sharpens our desires and makes us turn what we read into prayer. Listening to the Lord as He speaks to us in His word makes us pray for the blessings of which He speaks. When Christ spoke to the woman of Samaria about the living water, she exclaimed, "Give me this water." Pondering the promises of God's word makes us bold to plead them in a petition. When Elijah on Mount Carmel called upon Jehovah as the "God of Abraham, Isaac, and Israel," he claimed the covenanted promises given to the fathers that God would care for His people and indicate their cause against all the Lord's enemies. There is one incident recorded in the Acts of the Apostles which illustrates in a remarkable manner the separating influence of the word of God - when it is believed upon the life.

The Apostle Paul met with great success in his preaching at Ephesus. One result of his mission was that many who had used cunning arts burned all their books, and the cause of this is put down to the working of God's word.

For, in speaking of the burning of the books, it says, "So mightily grew the word of God and prevailed" (Acts 19:20). Let me take some time to inform my readers, that the word of God will separate the dirt of worldliness, the slime of unbelief, the mud of superstition, the filth of the lust, of the dust of conceit, the spots of jealousy and the ashes of pride.

When the Apostle Paul was leaving the Church in Ephesus, he said, "I commend you to God, and to the word of His grace, which is able to build you up" (Acts 20:23). God's word is given with authority and lodged with us as a trust. Not to obey the word of God is an act of rebellion.

The Bible is God's inspired revelation of the origin and destiny of all things. It is the power of God unto salvation and sources of present help for body, soul and spirit (Romans 1; 16, John 15:7). It is God's will to men in all ages, revealing the plans of God for man here and now and in the next life. It is the record of God's dealing with man- past, present, and future. It contains God's message of salvation to all who believe in Jesus Christ and of eternal damnation, the Bible is the most remarkable book ever made. It is a divine library of sixty-six books.

It is the book that contains the mind of God, the state of man, the way of salvation, the doom of sinners and the happiness of believers. Its doctrine is holy, its precepts binding, its histories true, and its decisions immutable. Therefore, read it to you be wise, believe it to be safe, and practice it to be holy. It contains light to direct you, food to support you, and comfort to cheer you. It is the traveler's map, the pilgrim's staff, the pilot's compass, the soldier's sword its decision and the Christian Charter. Here heaven is opened, and the gate of hell disclosed. Christ is its grand subject, our good is designed and the glory of God its end.

It should fill your memory, rule your heart, and guide your feet in righteousness and true holiness. Study it always, perseveringly, and industriously. It is a mine of wealth, the source of health and a world of pleasure. It is given to you in this life, will be opened at the judgment and will last forever. It involves the highest responsibility, will reward the least to the greatest labor and will condemn all who trifle with its sacred contents. It is a mirror to reflect (James 1:23); a hammer to convict (Jeremiah 23:29). A fire to refine, seed to multiply (1 Peter 1:23).

The Word

Much as our words reveal to others our hearts and minds, so Jesus Christ is God's "word" to reveal is His heart and mind to us. "He that hath seen me hath seen the Father." According to Hebrew's 1:1-3, Jesus Christ is God's last word to mankind, For He is the climax of divine revelation. Jesus Christ is the eternal Word (John 1:1-2). He existed in the beginning, not because He is eternal. He is God, and He was with God. "Before Abraham was, I am" (John 8:58).

Jesus Christ is the Creative Word

There is certainly a parallel between John 1:1 and Genesis 1:1 the "New Creation" and the "Old Creation." God created the world through His word: "And God said, "let there be..." For He spake, and it was done; He commanded, and it stood fast (Psalm33:9). God created all things by Himself, which means that Jesus is not a created being. He is eternal God. Jesus Christ is the eternal word. Jesus Christ is the incarnate word. He was not a phantom or a spirit when he ministered on earth, nor was His body a mere illusion. John and the other disciples each had a personal experience that convinced them of the reality of the body of Jesus (1 John1:1-2).
In his gospel, John points out that Jesus was weary (John 4:6) and thirsty (John4:7). He groaned within (John 11:33) and openly wept (John 11:35). On the cross, He thirsted (John19:28). After His resurrection, He proved to Thomas and the other disciples that He still had a real body (John 20: 24-29), howbeit, a glorified body. How was the word made flesh? By the miracle of the virgin birth (Isaiah 7:14 Matthew 1:18-25, Luke 1:26-32).

Jesus Is Essentially God

"And the word was God." That is, in His essence, in what He is, in His nature, person and personality of His attributes and character, Jesus is all that God is. He made all things, and without Him was not anything made that was made. All things, He took on Himself sinless human nature and identified with us in every aspect of life from birth to death. The word was not as an abstract concept of philosophy, but a real person who could be seen, touched and heard.

The plainest reason why the Son of God is called the word, seems to be, that as our words explain our minds to others. What John the evangelist says of Christ proves that He is God. He asserts, His essence in the beginning; the Word was made flesh. He made all things, and not as an instrument. Without Him was not anything made that was made, from the highest angel to the meanest worm. This shows how well qualified He was for the work of our redemption and salvation. The first verse of the Bible introduces God as the creator of the universe. The Bible does not try to prove that God exists. It assumes His existence as fundamental.

Creation itself bears witness that there is an intelligent, omnipotent, loving creator (Romans 1:20). The light of reason, as well as the life of sense, is derived from Christ and depends upon Him. The eternal Word, this true Light shines, but the darkness comprehends it not. In Him was life, and that life was the light of men. The light shines in the darkness, and the darkness has not overpowered it.

The Word made His dwelling among us. And the word was made flesh, and dwell among us, and we beheld his glory, the glory as of the only-begotten of the Father, full of grace and truth. No man hath seen God at any time; the only-begotten Son, which is in the bosom of the Father, He had declared Him. (John 1:14-18) Thy word has I hid in my heart, that I might not sin against thee (Psalm 119:11). The word of God is a most powerful antidote against sin when it has a place in the heart. Not only the precepts of it forbids but the promises of its influence and engage to a purity of the heart and life, and to the perfecting of holiness fear of the Lord; the word of God directs us in our work and way, and a dark place indeed the world be without it.

"Thy word is a lamp unto my feet," Solomon says of the law and commandment," the perceptive part of the word." Proverbs 6:23; this shows a man what is his duty, both towards God and man; by it is the knowledge of sin: this informs what righteousness. God requires of man, the Gospel part of the word is a great and glorious light. It is by this light that men come to have some knowledge of God in Christ. God is gracious and merciful in Christ. His person, offices, and grace of righteousness, salvation, and eternal life comes by Him.

"Thy word is a lamp unto my feet." We are walkers through the city of this world, and we are often called to go out unto its darkness; let us never venture there without the light-giving word, lest we slip with our feet. Each man should use the word of God personally, practically, and habitually, that he may see his way and see what lies in it. When darkness settles down upon all around me, the word of the Lord, like a flaming torch, reveals my way. God's word is a lamp by night, a light by day, and a delight at all times. He who walks in darkness is sure, sooner or later, to stumble; while he who walks by the light of day, or by the lamp of night, stumbleth not, but keep his uprightness (Gill's Exposition of the Entire Bible).

A word is composed of letters, and Jesus Christ is "Alpha and Omega" (Revelation 1:11). According to Hebrews 1:1-3, Jesus Christ is God's last word to humanity, for He is the climax of divine revelation. Jesus Christ is the Eternal Word (John 1:1-2). He existed in the beginning as a creature, but because He is eternal. He is God, and He is with God. "Before Abraham was, I am" (John 8:58). Be Alive God is Here (Warren W. Wiersbe).

God created all things through Jesus Christ (Colossians 1:16). The Apostle Paul says, "For by Him (Jesus Christ) were all things created, that are in the earth, visible and invisible, whether they be thrones, or dominions, or principalities, or power. All things were created by Him and for Him. He is before all things, and by Him, all things consist. He makes it clear that the Son of God came in the flesh and was subjected to the sinless infirmities of human nature. He took upon Himself sinless human nature and identified with us in every aspect of life from birth to death. "The Word" was not an abstract concept of philosophy, but a real person who could be seen, touched and heard. Jesus Christ revealed God's glory in His person, His works, and His words.

The people saw His works and heard his words. They observed His perfect life. He gave them every opportunity to grasp the truth, believe and be saved. Jesus is the way, but they would not walk with Him (John 6:66-71). He is the truth, but they would not believe Him. He is life, and they crucified Him!

Jesus Christ is the image of the invisible God and the firstborn of every creature (Colossians 1:15). "Who being the brightness of His glory, and the express image of his person, and upholding all things by the word of His power, when he had by Himself purged our sins, sat down on the right hand of the Majesty on high" (Hebrews 1:3). Jesus Christ was and is God in form. Deep, it would seem, in the constitution of the human soul, is the craving for some aspects of God. As Jesus Christ appears in the universe, He transcends the limits of human vision. He appears to His intelligent universe as well as to man.

"For the invisible things of Him from the creation of the world are clearly seen, being understood by the things that are made, even His eternal power and Godhead; so, that they are without excuse" (Romans 1:20). According to Psalm 138:2, David declares in his devotion, "I will worship towards thy holy temple, and praise thy name for thy loving kindness and for thy truth: for thou hast magnified thy Word above all thy name." Everything by which He has made Himself known in creation and providence; "Thou hast magnified thy word" all being done according to the word said in Himself, His decrees and purposes are declared in His word and promises, whereby He has glorified it. Jesus said "Sanctify them through thy truth: thy word is truth" (John 17:17). (The Gospel of John Expository and Homiletical Commentary by David Thomas).

The Christ of God Lived Among Men

This Christ life was a manifestation of Divine Glory to men. "We beheld His glory" Jehovah of the Old revealed Himself to His people in the mystic radiance of the Shekinah, but now in the Tabernacle or tent of Christ's humanity, He reveals Himself to the human race. The glory of God was seen in His dignified deportment, in His sublime doctrines, in His glorious deeds, but especially was it seen in His transfiguration. "We were eye witness of His Majesty," says Peter (2 Peter 1:16-17). He had flesh; He was made in all points like as we are; yet without sin.

Jesus Christ was something more than human nature. He was a man, but His humanity was only a constituent part of his personality. His humanity was no more Himself than the body of a man. Jesus was divine for the word that became flesh, we are told, was God.

There was no actual Christ in the universe until the incarnation, until the Word was made flesh." He is God communicated or interpreted into the visible human realm. As Jesus, Himself said, "If ye had known me, ye should have known my Father also: and from henceforth ye know him, and have seen him. He that hath seen me hath seen the Father" (John 14: 7-9). Paul, the apostle, wrote, "God was manifest in the flesh, justified in the Spirit, seen of angels, preached unto the Gentiles, believed on in the world, received up into glory" (I Timothy 1:16). His declaration is in perfect harmony with John 1:14 and 1 John 1:2. The Word is not a person distinct from God; the Word is God Himself. He expresses His mind verbally or in activity or in the incarnation. The word cannot be separated from God. Since Jesus is the Word made flesh, it is biblically accurate to say that Jesus is God Himself manifest in genuine human existence. Indeed, that is precisely what Scripture does say and what Jesus Christ Himself claimed.

In the statement "the word was made flesh" is a powerful testimony both to the Messiah's deity and His humanity. As the word, Jesus Christ is God. The Word of God does not have a personal identity separate from God, any more than the life of God has an identity separate from Him; as flesh Jesus Christ was a man. "Flesh" is a frequent metaphor for authentic and complete human existence.

To say "The word was made flesh" is striking. A.T. Robertson has pointed out that unless John was referring here to the virgin birth, the exact significance of 'made is beyond explanation (A.T. Robertson, Word Pictures in the New Testament). Indeed, John was referring to the virgin's birth, and his point was essentially the same as that of Galatians 4:4, "But when the fullness of time was come, God sent forth his Son, made of a woman, made under the law." Jesus, the Son of God, was made of (Greek, ek, "out of "or "from") a woman; That is, He received His human existence from Mary. The Messiah is divine by the fact that He had no human fathers; the Holy Spirit, which is the power of God caused Mary to conceive (Luke 1:31, 34-34). The Messiah is human by the fact that He did have a human mother; Mary conceived in her womb.

The Word Expressed In The Wisdom
and Counsel of His Will

God works "All things after the counsel of His own will." In whom also we have obtained an inheritance, being predestinated according to the purpose of Him who worketh all things after the counsel of His own will" (Ephesians 1:11). In Proverbs 8:22-31, Wisdom is personified as having been present with God at creation.

Wisdom is an attribute of God which has always been with Him. It should be noted that nowhere in the scripture is wisdom said to be the agent of creation. Instead, wisdom is said to have been present when the LORD Himself accomplished the work of creation. Since God created by His word, this scripture indicates that the wisdom of God was expressed by His creative words. This is in perfect harmony with John 1:3, 10: All this were made by Him, and without Him was not anything made that was made, and the world was made by Him. Therefore, since Jesus is the Word made flesh, it is no marvel to discover that He is the very wisdom of God made known to man (1 Corinthians 1:24; Colossians 2:3).

The heart of scripture is "The Word of God." Our Lord became incarnate in human flesh, with the weakness and needs of human nature. There is a sense, therefore, in which we may say that in the Holy Scripture, the Word has become flesh and tabernacles among us.

The Bible is a spiritual Book. Christ declares, "The words that I speak unto you, they are spirit, and they are life" (John 6:63); and further, we are reminded that the word of God is living (Hebrews 4:12). The Word is Christ and the Word not only contains life or a medium of life; it is life.

The Imperial Dictionary says: "The Bible is the sacred scriptures of the Old and New Testament, as received by the Christian Church as a Divine Revelation." "The scriptures are the Divine breathing." Our English word "inspired" occurs in one other place, and that is (Job 32:8-9). "But there is a spirit in man: and the inspiration of the Almighty giveth them understanding."

Great men are not always wise: neither do the aged understand judgment. Therefore: as God breathed into man the breath of life and he became a living soul, so God has breathed this book, and it breathes out what He has breathed.

It breathes life into the spirit, love into the soul, understanding into the mind, determination into the will, grace into the heart, beauty into the life, and harmony into the being. "Holy men of God spake as they were moved by the Holy Ghost" (2 Peter 1:21). These men were in fellowship with God; Holy men and the Holy Spirit needed to be in touch with each other to produce holy results.

The word "moved" means to be "borne along" and is used for a ship being "driven" by the wind (Acts 27:17); of a man being brought on a bed (Luke 5:18); and one who is carrying another (John 21:18). This at once makes the Bible different from all other books.

Chapter 6

The Priority of Morality

There is a fundamental question we all have to face. How are we to live our lives; by what principles and moral values will be guided and inspired? (William A. Dembski). Today we are afraid of simple words like goodness and mercy and kindness, writes Lin Yutang. "We don't believe in the good old values anymore. And that is why the world is so sick." A thing that will help your inner life is to set up in your mind a standard of values so that you know what is significant, important and valuable. Conduct is life in the long run happiness, and prosperity depends upon it. Eternal circumstances are of comparatively little importance; it does not so much matter what surrounds us, as what we are. Right and wrong are in the nature of things. They are not words and phrases. They are in the nature of things, and if you by any means transgress the law laid down, imposed by the nature of things, depend upon it you will pay the penalty (John Morley).

There is an underlying pattern of law which establishes what is moral and what is not. What is good conduct and what is not. Regardless of the systems man builds up for himself nationally or religiously, there is still a system of laws which work to produce penalties for normal actions. In reality, says C.S. Lewis, "Moral rules are directions for running the human machine. Every moral rule is there to prevent a breakdown, or strain, or friction, in running that machine. That is why these rules at first seem to be constantly interfering with our natural inclination."

Motives are invisible, but they are the true test of character. Behavior is a mirror in which everyone shows his image. Throughout life, we are always called upon to make decisions involving the distinction between right and wrong decisions which in no way injure our fellow man, while producing satisfactory results for ourselves.

We learn that certain laws govern our acts and that certain results inevitability follow their performance. It's certainly a worthy thing when people passes character so impeccable that they can't be accused of doing wrong except in matters relating to their faith. As you take a stand for what is morally right, and what Lord has commanded you to do, you will be falsely accused cruelly persecuted and justly killed. "Yes, and all who desire to live godly in Christ Jesus will suffer persecution" (2 Timothy 3:12). The moral sense is more important than intelligence. When it disappears from a nation, the whole social structure slowly commences crumbling away. History reveals nations rise and fall, but the moral law is written on the tables of eternity. Moral rules are directions for running the human machine, and never hurting others. Everyone is indebted to the church and every nation. Organization and person who uplifted the moral standards of man. However, most of us learn our moral values in the church. The very foundation of a man, and that which is the mightiest moving force of his life, and must be, is the moral quality of his being.

"America has cast off her moral guidelines and is adrift in a sea of immorality and crime and sensuality that threatens our very permanence," writes (Dr. E. Palen). Fundamentally, the force that rules the world is conduct, whether it be moral or immoral, there is only no hope, but no prospect of anything but destruction of all that has been accomplished during the last 5000 years. Passions are vices or virtues in their highest powers. Therefore, to control our passions, we must govern our habits, and keep watch over ourselves in the small details of everyday life. The happiness of a man in this life does not consist in the absence but the mastery of passions. The code by which we live becomes the code which may cause our death. No one can be well or happy who is troubled by his conduct.

Humanity has its richest flavor; home is most peaceful and happy, and human rights are most peaceful and happy, and human rights are most fully regarded. When any community is most completely under the power of a spiritual life; All forms of evil are lessened, and vice hides its deformed head. Morality as virtues suggests that the morality of a person depends on the traits and temperaments that he or she possesses and values. You see, moral desires, and integrity will always have the capability for a person to behave honorably by the hierarchical order of virtues.

He believed that the highest and complex of virtues are expressed by the concept of willpower while the lowest and simplistic of virtues are expressed by the concept of integrity. This began with early philosophers such as Aristotle, Plato, and Socrates. They believed that "To know good is to do the good." Therefore, Morality may also be specifically synonymous with goodness and rightness. One of the main questions within the psychological study of morality is the issue of what qualitatively distinguishes moral attitudes from non-moral attitudes. Moral philosophy includes moral ontology, or the origin of morals, as well as morals epistemology, or what is known about moral. Different systems of expressing morality have been proposed, including deontological ethical systems which adhere to a set of established rules, and normative ethical systems which consider the merits of actions themselves. An example of normative ethical philosophy is the golden rule which states that "One should treat others as one would like others to treat oneself. How do we evaluate morality? First, Immorality is the active opposition to morality, opposition to that which is good or right; While amorality is defined as an unawareness of, indifference toward, or disbelieve in any set of moral standards. According to the Westminster Dictionary of Christian Ethics, religion and morality are to be defined differently and have no definitional connections with each other.Let's take a look at moral behavior. First, we must ask, what are some examples of moral behavior? Moral behavior is subjective, but it is represented by an individual's knowledge of social and cultural norms and the capacity to perform good works through selfless actions. Therefore, some moral behaviors may include honestly, giving to charity and avoiding negative situations. Moral, ethical virtuous, righteous, noble mean conforming to a standard of what is right and good. Moral implies conformity to established sanctioned codes or acceptable notions of right and wrong. Ethical may suggest the involvement of more difficult or subtle questions of righteousness, fairness, or equity.

Moral Decision About Sin

Knowing this, that our old man is crucified with him, that the body of sin might be destroyed, that henceforth we should not serve sin (Romans 6:6).

It takes a long time to come to a moral decision about sin; sin must die out in us, not be curbed or suppressed or counteracted but crucified. We may be earnestly convinced, and religiously convinced, but what we need to do is to come to the decision which Paul forces here. Haul, pick yourself up, take time alone with God, make the moral decision and say, "Lord, identify me with thy death until I know that sin is dead in me." Make the moral decision that sin in you must be put to death. It was not a divine anticipation on the part of Paul, but a very radical and definite experience. Are you prepared to let the Spirit of God search your heart, and soul until you know what the disposition of sin is, the thing that lusts against the Spirit of God in you? Then if so will you agree with God's verdict on that disposition of sin, that it should be identified with death of Jesus? You cannot reckon yourself dead indeed unto sin unless you have been through this radical issue of will before God. Have you entered into the glorious privilege of being crucified with Christ until all that is left is the life of Christ in your flesh and blood? "I am crucified with Christ nevertheless I live; yet not I, but Christ liveth in me.

"Apart from values and ethics which I have tried to live by, the legacy I would like to leave behind is a very simple one, that I have always stood up for what I consider to be the right thing, and I have tried to be as fair and equitable as I could be" (Ratan Tata). Our success in the persuasion of life comes from how we merge the activities and actions of our moral stands. "For God, holy wrath and indignation are revealed from heaven against all ungodliness and unrighteousness of men, who in their wickedness repress and hinder the truth and make it inoperative (Romans 3:18). Who shall be punished with over lasting destruction from the presence of the Lord, and from the glory of His power, (2 Thessalonians 1:9). Moses God's prophet says, "The Lord saw that the wickedness of man was great in the earth and that every imagination and intention of all human thinking was only evil continually." And the Lord regretted that He had made man on the earth, and He was grieved at heart (Genesis 6: 5-6 AMP). Sentence every immoral thought for detention and prosecution. Immorality is a powerful gadget that brings down great monuments of success. Don't entertain immorality. According to Romans 6: 11-14, The Apostle Paul tells us, "Likewise reckon ye also yourselves to be dead indeed unto sin, but alive unto God through Jesus Christ our Lord.

The Priority of Morality

Let not sin therefore reign in your mortal body, that ye should obey it in the lusts thereof. Neither yield ye your members as instruments of unrighteousness unto sin: but yield yourselves unto God, as those that are alive from the deeds, and your members as instruments of righteousness unto God.

For sin shall not have dominion over you: For ye are not under the law but grace. Paul says, "Present your members as servants to unrighteousness." There is something we have to do. Man's soul is weak enough to yield to influence but strong enough not to yield all at once." "Freedom of the will" (A phrase) this is a catch phrase that has more of error than of truth in it. We are all so made that we can yield to influence that is brought to bear upon us, and if we keep ourselves long enough under right influences, we shall find that we can form habits that will develop us along the line of those influences. The peculiarity of the moral habits, distinguishing them from the intellectual acquisition, is the presence of two hostile powers. One to be gradually raised into the ascendant over the other. It is necessary, above all things, in such a situation, never to lose a battle. Every gain on the wrong side undoes the effect of many conquests on the right. Let's take a look at Genesis 6: 5-6. God saw that the wickedness of man was great in the earth and that every imagination of the thoughts of his heart was only evil continually. And it repented the Lord that He had made man on the earth, and it grieved Him at His heart. The earth also was corrupt before God, and the earth was filled with violence. So, God looked upon the earth, and indeed it was corrupt, for all flesh had corrupted their way on the earth. In another word, the moral standard of earth was certainly corrupted. God said to Noah, "The end of all flesh has come before me, for the earth is filled with violence through them; and behold, I will destroy them with the earth" (Genesis 6:13). The most remarkable thing concerning the old world is the destroying of it by the deluge or flood. We are told of the abounding iniquity of that wicked world. God's just wrath, and His holy resolution to punish it (Matthew Henry's Concise Commentary; Oswald Chambers, 1936; The Moral Foundation of Life).

The Lord declared that His Spirit should not thus strive with men always. He would leave them out to be hardened in sin, and ripened for destruction.

This He determined on because man was flesh; not only frail and feeble but carnal and depraved; having misused the noble powers of his soul to gratify his corrupt inclinations. The wickedness of people is great indeed when noted sinners are men renowned among them. Grievous sin was committed in all places, by all sorts of people. The masses forbade the priority of morality. Anyone might see that the wickedness of man was great. But God saw that every imagination, or purpose, of the thoughts of man's heart, was only evil continually. This was the bitter root, the corrupt spring. The heart was deceitful and desperately wicked; the principles were corrupt; the habits and dispositions evil. Their designs and devices were wicked. They did evil deliberately, contriving how to make mischief. There was no good among them. God saw man's wickedness as one injured and wronged by it. He saw it as a tender father sees the folly and stubbornness of a rebellious and disobedient child, which grieves Him, and makes Him wish He has been childless. Oh, that we may look on Him whom we have grieved, and mourn! God repented that he had made man, but we never find Him repent that He redeemed man. He resolved to destroy man: the original word is very striking, "I will wipe off man from the earth; as dirt or filth is wiped off from a place which should be cleaned and is thrown to the dunghill, the proper place for it." God speaks of man as His own creature, when He determined is punishment. They forfeit their lives who do not answer the end of their living. God speaks of resolution concerning men after His Spirit had been long striving with them in vain. None are punished by the justice of God, but those who hate to be reformed by the grace of God. Achieving your happiness is the only moral purpose of your life, and that happiness, not pain or mindless self-indulgence, is the proof of your moral integrity since it is the proof and result of your loyalty to the achievement of your value (Ayn Rand; Gill's Exposition of the Entire Bible).

The effective management of morality is one of the most difficult and yet critical aspects of effective global management. Making the right moral decisions can be challenging in the best of circumstances. Internationally, the difficulties increase exponentially. While national managers inevitably address moral issues, global managers confront them more frequently and deal with dilemmas that are more difficult to resolve. One should realize that ethics focuses on the study of morals and moral choices and governs personal and company behaviors.

The Priority of Morality

Culture impacts moral norms because culture is inherent value centered. And so, one may find that moral behavior may be perceived as inappropriate as another. Cultures also change over time, and in some countries, values are changing more rapidly than in others. In ancient time, it took hundreds and in some cases thousands of years before practices such as human sacrifices and slavery were viewed as unjust or immoral. In modern times, the ethical and moral issues vary and are subject to more change.

Woe unto them that call evil good, and good evil; that put darkness for light, and light for darkness; that put bitter for sweet, and sweet for bitter! (Isaiah 5:20).

Ye have wearied the Lord with your words. Yet ye say, "Wherein have we wearied Him? When ye say, everyone that doeth evil is good in the sight of the Lord, and He delighteth in them; or where is the God of Judgment? (Malachi 2:17).

Who knoweth the judgment of God, that they which commit such things are worthy of death, not only do the same but have pleasure in them that do them (Romans 1:32).

There is no lasting happiness in morality, which have built great men and women and point the way to which one may find. Each day we are becoming a creature of splendid glory or one of unthinkable horror (C.S. Lewis). Mortify therefore your members which are upon the earth; fornication, uncleanness, inordinate affection, evil concupiscence, and covetousness, which is idolatry (Colossians 3:5).

Chapter 7

You Must Wrestle to Survive

Finally, my brethren, be strong in the Lord, and in the power of His might. Put on the whole armor of God, that we may be able to stand against the wiles of the devil (Ephesians 6: 10-11). To put on the armor of God is to appropriate this power in our lives. Paul tells us: by wearing God's armor, how we wrestle not against flesh and blood, but against principalities, against powers, against the rulers of the darkness of this world, against spiritual wickedness in high places.

Too many people waste their lives away, wishing the way to heaven were easier but unwilling to get busy and seek the grace they need for such an enterprise. They need to see that wrestling for the Lord promises a sure victory; while wrestling against Him is a sure guarantee of defeat. The mystery of the damned will be compounded when they fully understand what they lost in disobeying God. Then they will remember all the means once offered them which could have gotten them eternal life. When it is too late, they will regret that they had no desire to take Christ's offer. There are those who only pretend to wrestle. Other individuals make a lot of noise about their religion; but who secretly have their hearts set on earthly goals. They pretend to be heaven - bound, but their hearts are full of hypocrisy. Such deceivers are like the eagle, who, when he soars highest, has his eye fixed on his prey below. Life is not a picnic but a conflict. Therefore, it is necessary that we anticipate the days before us. There be foes that we contend with that are not humans but superhuman (Ephesians 6:12). This unseen intelligence is not the creation of the Jewish fancy but is an object of revelation.

Principalities, powers, rulers of the darkness of this world, and spiritual hosts of wickedness in the heavenly places are personal forces, vast in numbers and highly organized. They may work through human agencies, but they are our real foes. Do we ever give them a thought? Superhuman enemies cannot be defeated by human means, and so provision is divinely made. Scriptures promises, "The people that do know their God shall be strong and do exploits" (Daniel 11:32). An angel told Daniel which men would stand up and be counted for God when tempted and persecuted by Antiochus. Some would be taken in by the bribery of corrupt men; others would fall victim to intimidation and threats, but a few who were firmly grounded in the tenets of their faith, would do great things for God. That is to say, to flatteries they would be incorruptible, and to power and force unconquerable. The forces of evil are spiritual forces of wickedness. They seek to receive the loyalty and devotion that is due to God. Therefore, they desire to control the spirit of man; that part of man that is destined to worship and serve God and exist forever. If they can capture the spirit of man, they have him eternally... his life and presence forever. Therefore, these beings attempt all they can do to lead humanity into wickedness. Some persons have scoffed at the idea of a personal devil or demons who exist in a so-called spiritual world. They feel that they are too educated and intellectual to believe such nonsense. They proclaim that such ideas are outdated and belong to the dark ages of man's ignorance and super-stitions. But note a significant fact: man, is ever so conscious of what he terms: Sub-conscious horrors that affect both his mind and body; Unseen and uncomfortable forces that affect his behavior;

Cosmic forces that affect and determine his behavior; Blind faith that controls his life like a puppet. Satan and his demonic forces rank among the highest angel- princes in the hierarchy of the heavenly places, yet all of them owe their existence to Christ, through whom they were created (Colossians 1:16), and who is accordingly the head of all principalities and powers. These demonic forces have embarked upon rebellion against God. They not only seek to force humankind to give them the worship that is due to Him but launched an assault upon the crucified Christ at a time when these spirits thought they had Him at their mercy. But, far from suffering their attack without resistance, Christ grappled with them and overcame them, stripping them of their armor and conquering them in His triumphal procession (Colossians 2:15).

Thus, the hostile powers of evil which you must encounter are already vanquished powers.

Think for a moment and be honest. Think of all the wickedness and evil, wrong doing and selfishness in the world, all the division, anger, prejudice, favoritism, hate, pride, war, killing lying, stealing, arrogance, cursing, selfishness, immorality, bitterness. The list could go on and on ad infinitum. The evil of man consumes the news reports every day. Just think about it.

Do we not know better? Do not enough of us know better? Enough of us that we could change things? Yes, we do. Why then do we not change the world? The passage tells us why: "For we wrestle not against flesh and blood, but against principalities, against powers, against the rulers of the darkness of this world, against spiritual wickedness in his place" (Ephesians 6:12).

God - because He is God, has to tell us the truth. He cannot do otherwise. Therefore, God reveals to us a fact that is as clearly evident in any other single event on earth. There is an evil force that has access to the spirit of man and can influence and enslave man to do evil. He is called Satan, who rules over the darkness and spiritual wickedness of this world. The only hope for God's children is to put on the whole armor of God; please remember, that our warfare is not human or physical, but spiritual. Oliver Wendell Home wrote," If I had a formula for bypassing trouble, I wouldn't pass it around. Wouldn't be doing anybody a favor. Trouble creates a capacity to handle it. I don't say embrace trouble. That's as bad as treating it as an enemy. But I do say meet it as a friend. For you will see a lot of it and better be on speaking terms with it."

The Christian's Call to Courage

This is the way to cultivate courage: first, by standing firm on some conscientious principle, some law of duty. Next, by being faithful to the truth and right on small occasions and common events. Third, by trusting God for help and power (J.F. Clarke).

"In our wrestling match with our foes. We must be very courageous." Are you facing as enemy today? Take your hands off the problem and let God deal with those who are involved. He will remedy the problem in the best way possible. A cowardly spirit is beneath the lowest duty of a Christian. You of all persons will need courage and determination if you hope to obey your heavenly captain's orders. He commands us, "Be thou strong and very courageous... why? So, you can stand in battle against hostile nations? So, you can make a great name for yourself? No! But that thou mayest observe to do accordingly to all the law, which Moses my servant commanded thee (Joshua 1:7).

God's church is a militant host. The church warfare is with unseen forces of evil. God's people compose an army fighting to establish His kingdom on the earth. This army is to destroy the sovereignty of Satan and over its ruins, erect the kingdom of God, which is "Righteousness, and peace, and joy in the Holy Ghost" (Romans 14:17). This militant army is composed of individual soldiers of the cross. The armor of God is needed for defense and added prayer crowns to the entire army. The battle is not altogether a personal matter. Victory cannot be achieved for self alone. There is a sense in which the entire army of Christ is involved (E.M. Bounds).

When Satan comes to tempt you, observe your behavior. How do you respond to his enticement? Do you stand fast on the ordinances of God and refuse to be swayed? Or does your soul embrace the temptation as a bosom friend, glad for an excuse to entertain it? If so you are under the power of Satan! In the words of Paul, know ye not, that to whom ye yield yourself servants to obey, his servants ye are? (Romans 6:16). Have you joined the troops that fight to subdue the insurrections of evil spurred on by Satan? Just standing on the sideline and cheering other Saints to victory is not enough. Join in the race that is ahead.

Be always mindful, that "our wrestling is against the principalities, the powers against the world rulers of this darkness, against the spiritual hosts of wickedness in the heavenly places". Paul says our hand-to-hand fighting is not against flesh and blood; that is not the realm of our conflict. They beat Paul with stripes; He did not resist.

When they put Him in the stocks, with his body lacerated, leaving stigma upon Him; Paul did not resist. He recognized the whole realm of the underworld of evil spirits under the mastery of Satan and creating the natural antagonisms.

Therefore, beloved, given that conflict we have received a mandate Divine order, 'Put on the whole armor of God". It is self-evident that there is a difference between putting on and taking up. Putting on is dressing for a parade while taking up is for actual conflict. Paul's description of the armor is graphic. Truth for the loins, righteousness for the breastplate, readiness in the gospel of peace for the feet, faith for the shield, salvation for the helmet, the word of God for the sword, prayer and supplication which make the armor effective. The expression "the whole armor of God" is in itself a remarkable one.

In a letter explaining the hope and purpose behind the great system of scholarships, he was creating, Cecil Rhodes wrote that when he was seeking was not merely bookworms, but the best man for the world's fight. The longer one lives on this troubled planet, the plainer it becomes that "whether we like it or not—all of us are engaged in a ceaseless war, the endless struggle between love and hate, good and evil, truth and lies, freedom and tyranny. Each of us has a thousand private battlefields. And the happiest people, it seems to me, are those who fight the hardest." (Arthur Gordon).

A Word of Encouragement to Wrestlers

Perhaps you are discouraged, not only by the strength of the enemy but by your apparent weakness and the constant contention with sin and self. Be encouraged! There is strong consolation for God's children who struggles with the truth of God's grace and their inner conflicts with sin. Gideon cried out in despair, "if the Lord be with us, why is all this befallen us? (Judges 6:13).

We understand his perplexity because we identify with his sufferings. Our hearts, too cry out, "why do I find such struggling in me, provoking me to sin, pulling me back from that which is good?

God has a ready answer if we will stop whining long enough to hear it. Because he says, "you are a wrestler, not a conqueror." Too often we mistake the state of a child of God in this life. He is not immediately called to triumph over his enemies but is carried into battle to fight them. Therefore, God, Himself will enter the battle in disguise and appear to be your enemy, rather than leave no enemy for you to wrestle.

When Jacob was alone, he sent a man to wrestle with him until dawn. Take comfort in the fact that you are a wrestler. The Christian's wrestling against the powers of darkness is no less desperate and fateful. The point to see is that the believer's struggle is not against flesh and blood. Let's not forget;" His foes are not human but physical." They are spiritual forces that possess incredible powers. Note what has said: the believer fights against principalities, against powers, against rulers of darkness, against spiritual wickedness. This reveals some very clear things to us.

1. The forces of evil are powerful forces.
2. The forces of evil are numerous. Principalities, powers, rulers all con vey the idea of a vast number of evil forces that are struggling against the believer.
3. The forces of evil are organized similarly to a government or a hierarchy of evil.

Against, principalities, powers, and rulers of this world in high places… all point toward a ranking of spiritual forces with enormous authority, position, and rule. Many challenging and dangerous men opposed Paul and tried to destroy his influence and defeat his purpose. Nevertheless, God's children must never compromise with Satan, even though his promise may be very attractive. The fight against him must be continuous and strenuous. "We wrestle." It is wise to remember that Satan never retreats willingly. He never vacates a human soul until the incoming power of God expels him. To nullify his efforts, the children of the Lord needs every assistance possible. Paul knew this fact and proceeded to explain each detail of the protection supplied by his commander-in-chief. Properly clothed and suitably arrayed, the redeemed warrior may confidently move to the battlefield.

"Wherefore take unto you the whole armor of God that ye may be able to withstand in the evil day and having done all to stand. He was not asked to win a battle, but preserve that which had been won by the Savior. "the battle is not yours, but the Lord's" (2 Chronicles 20:15). To be able to stand against the wiles of the devil would be their greatest achievement. Looking too much at Satan is dangerous. He has the hypnotic ability to paralyze souls and destroy their defenses. It is better to emulate the example given by David, who stated, "I will lift up mine eyes unto the hills from whence cometh my help. My help cometh from the Lord, which made heaven and earth" (Psalm 122:1-2). Since the Lord always goes before His people into danger, His presence is between Satan and vulnerable souls. God's nearness is the guarantee of safety; He stands between His children and the enemy. When Christians deviate from their appointed places of duty and turn either to the right or left, they become easy targets for "the fiery darts of the wicked ones."

When the enemies attack Roman soldiers, the soldiers formed themselves into human squares with men facing in every direction. If a soldier fell, another one from inside the formation took the place of the fallen comrade. Their greatest duty at that time was not to advance but to stand. More often than not, the attacks of the enemies were defeated because defenders refused to retreat. The apostle apparently had such in mind when he urged his friends to stand together. Each faithful Christian would support and strengthen his comrades, and the unified purpose of the entire company would guarantee victory.

Victories That Are Easy and Cheap

"Those only are worth having which come as the result of hard fighting" (H.W. Beacher). There is a continuous need for every individual in God's army to be steadfast, for only then would victory be assured. God's children should anticipate how and when and an attack may be launched and be ready to offset the onslaught. To forestall the devil's plan and thwart his efforts is the forerunner of victory. The devil is cunning and crafty; he possesses ways to overcome his opposition. Realizing this, Paul urged readers to put on the whole armor of God, an action made possible by the Savior.

To be satisfied with just a part of what God supplied is the epitome of stupidity. "For we wrestle not against flesh and blood, but against principalities, against powers, against rulers of the darkness of this world, against spiritual wickedness in high places (Ephesians 6:12).

In this directive from the Apostle Paul, we have been challenged to be strong. Finally, be strong in the Lord and in his great power. Put on the full armor of God so that you can fight against the devil's evil trickery. Our battle is not against people on earth but the rulers and authorities and the powers of this world's darkness. Against the spiritual forces of evil in the heavenly world. That is why you need to put on God's full armor. Then on the day of evil, you will be able to stand strong: and when you have finished the whole fight, you will still be standing. So, stand firm, with the belt of truth, girt around your waist and the protection of right living on your chest. On your feet wear the good news of peace to help you stand strong. And also, use the shield of faith with which you can stop all the burning arrows of the evil one. Accept God's salvation as your helmet, and take the sword of the Spirit, which is the word of God (Ephesians 6: 10-1; The Everyday Bible New Century Version). God's children are not to attack Satan, or advance against him; they are only to "stand" or hold the territory Christ and His body, the church, have conquered. Without God's armor, His children will be defeated by the schemes of the devil which have been effective for thousands of years. For the sake of emphasis: Be reminded that the struggle is not physical against flesh and blood; it is a spiritual conflict against the religious "MAFIA" Therefore, be prepared. You're up against far greater than you can handle on your own. Take all the help you can get, every weapon God has issued, so that when it's all over but the shouting, you'll still be on your feet.

Chapter 8

The Power of Choice

What a thrilling success story Joseph's is! From earliest years, his rise from a pit to Pharaoh's palace has fascinated us. What a rags-to-riches story his is! Sold as a slave to Potiphar's house, Joseph personality soon impressed the household, particular the wife of Potiphar. She, with all the lustfulness of Egyptian women, conceived a passion for Joseph's beauty and physique and tempted him. Had he yielded to animal appetites, he would have lost a glorious future, and above all his regard for God. So, the story is related in manner. The pious youth flatly rejected his mistress base proposal to sin with her. With abhorrence, Joseph knew what would be involved in yielding to her enticements. He could not betray his trust and act in such a vile and ungrateful manner toward his master. How could he do this great wickedness and sin against God?

"God always give His best to those who leave the choice with him. It is not who you are that hold you back; it's who you think you are not. When you have to make a choice, and don't make it, that is in itself a choice." Unknown

Years passed on, and Joseph became the standard and bailiff in his master's house. Pharaoh left all that he had in Joseph's hand; and he knew not aught he had, save the bread which he did eat. "And it was just here that Joseph encountered the most terrible temptation of his life. We may expect temptation in days of prosperity and ease rather than in those of privation and toil. It is easy to keep the armor on when we ascend the desolate mountain pass, struggling against the cold blast, and afraid that any boulder may hide an assassin. It is hard to keep it buckled close when we have reached the happy valley, with its good air. A temptation is harder to resist

Egyptian women in those days employed as much liberty as some of our women do nowadays; the Egyptian monuments has proven this. It also testifies to the extreme laxity of their morals. It may be that Potiphar's wife was not worse than many of her gender, though we blush to read of her great proposals.

The ship that passes in the night, and speaks to each other in passing; only a signal shown and a distant voice in the darkness. So, in the ocean of life, we pass and speak to one another, only a look and a voice, then darkness again and silence (Henry Wordsworth Longfellow).

The immediate appeal to Joseph's passion invested the temptation tenfold. Not all struggles come with a warning. For example; the sailor is warned of the burning storm; but alas for him if a sudden squall catches him! Friend, beware of sudden squall! Policy and conscience are often at variance with temptation. It seemed essential for Joseph to be in good stead with his master's wife. To please her would secure his advancement. To cross her would make her foe and ruin his hopes.

"He who cannot resist temptation is not a man. Whoever yields to temptation debases himself with a debasement from which he can never arise." (Horace Mann). The only armor against the policy is faith that looks to the long future and believes that in the end it would be found better to have done right and to have waited for the vindication and blessing of God. Joseph did not heed to the suggestions of policy; If he had done so, he might have acquired a little more influence in the house of Potiphar. This influence could not have lasted, and he would never have become Prime Minister of Egypt. Joseph would never have a long home of his own or have brought his sons to receive the blessing of his dying father. There were peculiar elements of trial in Joseph's case. Opportunity accompanied the temptation "There were none of the men of the house there within." It was well timed, and if he had yielded, there was not much fear of detection and punishment; the temptress would never publish her shame. The temptation that tries to win its way by its very importunity is to be feared most of all. Joseph stood firm. He reasoned with her. Joseph referred to his master's kindness and trust. He held up the confidence that he dared not betray.

He brought the case from the court of reason to that of conscience, and asked in words forever memorable, and which have given the secret of victory to tempted souls in all ages: "How then can I do this great wickedness, and sin against God." If history teaches anything, it teaches that sensual indulgence is the surest way to national ruin. The temptation of our great cities is too many and vigorous for the young to resist. Joseph knew that God had been behind all that had been happening; when he had been lied on by Potiphar's wife. He could now see that God had overruled. No one could have told him that at the time. But now he could see a stupendous moment had come. He was standing before Pharaoh. How could he have engineered that? God had done it. God had been behind it all so that he could say that God had engineered the worst thing that had ever happened to him. God will bring us to that place also. Joseph's spiritual strength was affirmed. Pharaoh confirmed his spiritual strength when he said, "Can we find such a one as this, a man in whom the Spirit of God is? (Genesis 41:38). The character of Joseph was placed on the line. Accused of immorality, put in prison; but look at (Genesis 41:39), Pharaoh said unto Joseph, "Forasmuch as God had shown thee all this, there is none so discreet and wise as thou art." Potiphar's wife has accused Joseph of an indiscretion. Then Pharaoh came along and said, "There's none so discreet as you." If you have been lied about on a large scale or a lesser scale and you are at work trying to vindicate yourself, remember that "he that looseth his life shall find it." Therefore, let God do it. He will do it in the most unexpected way. For some folks in this life, "it's humiliation today, exaltation tomorrow. Pharaoh said to Joseph, I've set you over the land of Egypt. Pharaoh charged Joseph, "I am Pharaoh, and without thee shall no man lift up is hand or foot in all the land of Egypt. Nothing gives God greater pleasure than vindicating his word.

Temptations are as thick as leaves of the forest, and no one can be out of the reach of temptation unless he is dead (Robert G. Ingersoll).

Every conquering temptation represents a new fund of moral energy. Every trial endured and weathered in the right spirit makes a soul nobler and stronger than it was before. (William Butler Yeats).

With my faith at my back pushing me, I will not give in. Upon the wings of angels carrying me, I will never let evil win. And though at times darkness surrounds me. I will always find light with God in my corner, no punch the devil lands on me will make me lose and fight. (Eugene N. Butler).

Your personal values are not just what espouse. It is how you behave and react in the face of temptation, under pressure, even when you know that no one else would know (K.S. Venkatraman).

Take every moment in your stride to make it worth a treasure of life. It is never too late to be what you are destined for only it matters how you take the moment and make it beautiful (Dr. Anil K.R. Sinha).

Joseph's Last Days and Death

In the competitive world of business where it is every man for himself, where only the most ruthless succeed, it is a great comfort to know that God has a plan for our lives. While other men claw, and scratch their way to the top, the children/people of the Lord simply rest in the knowledge that "the Lord will fulfill His purpose for us." O that each of us may go on shining more and more each day until our last, and that, when heart and flesh are failing most conspicuously, the life of the spirit may flash out with its most brilliant lights. It was under all these circumstances that Joseph said, "God will surely visit you, and ye shall carry up my bones from hence." (Genesis 50:25).

Potiphar's wife probably arranged for the other servants to be out of the way the day she launched her immoral plan, but at the same time she saw to it that servants were near enough at hand for her to call so, they would see Joseph's garment. There are times when fleeing could be a mark of cowardice (Psalm 11:1-2); Nehemiah 6:11), but there are also times when fleeing is evidence of courage and integrity. Joseph was wise enough to follow the same advice Paul gave to Timothy, "Flee the evil desires of youth" (2 Timothy 2:22 NIV).

Self-respect is the root of discipline: The sense of dignity grows with the ability to say no to oneself (Abraham Joshua Herschel).

Self-Aid, "Asking counsel of one that had a familiar spirit" (I Chronicles 10:13). Know how to choose well. Most of life depends on thereon. It needs good taste and correct judgment, for which neither intellect nor study suffices. To be a choice, you must choose, and for this two things are needed to be able to choose at all and then to choose the best (Gracian). At one time Saul's conviction was deep, yet he perished at last in his iniquity. It is real life to those who pursue their destiny (Paulo Coelho). How tragic was the end of Saul! Samuel withdrew his presence and influence. The spirits anointing was removed. The King because the victim of mental disturbances which the harp of David occasionally calmed. He patronized the witchcraft he once condemned and died by his hand. The youth of enormous stature who commenced his reign with great promise died 40 years later as a sinner and suicide.

"While we are free to choose our actions, we are not free to choose the consequences of our actions." (Stephen Covey).

"In the long run, we shape our lives, and we shape ourselves. The process never ends until we die. And the choices we make are ultimately our responsibility." Eleanor Roosevelt.

Saul was one of the most pathetic, most tragic, and most mysterious of Bible personalities. God came upon Saul for outward and earthly acts, but never for an inward change of hearts. The anointed King of Israel had neither part nor lot in the actual kingdom of God. As trials and temptations beset Saul, because of his hard and stony heart, a spirit of rebellion, and pride, jealousy, and despair took possession of him. The Spirit held him to his terrible end. The man had no deep-seated religious principle, no fear of God that influenced his life. His day began in bright sunshine; by noon thick clouds began to gather, and night overtook him in a tempest of tragedy. His remarkable rise passed through a decaying reign to last rain.

"The wrath of God is like great waters that are dammed for the present. They increase more and more, and rise higher and higher, till an outlet is given. The longer the stream is stopped, the more rapid and mighty its course, when once it is let loose. It's true that judgment against your evil work has not been executed. The flood of God's vengeance has been withheld, but your guilt in the meantime is constantly increasing.

You are treasuring up more wrath; the waters are continually rising and waxing more and more. There is nothing but more pleasure of God that holds the waters back that are unwilling to be stopped, and press hard to go forward. If God should only withdraw his hand from the floodgate, it would immediately fly open, and the fiery floods of the fierceness and wrath of God would rush forth with inconceivable fury. It would come upon you with omnipotent power. If your strength were ten thousand times greater than it is, you, the thousand times greater than the strength of the stoutest, sturdiest devil in hell, it would be nothing to withstand or endure it." (Sinners in the hand of the angry God by Jonathan Edwards).

It is the fact that gives rise to all that follows; souls blameless suspicion, his bitter jealousy, his cruel vengeance, and his periodic madness. The good spirit left him, and an evil spirit took possession of him, and at the end, he was without help or hope. There was no Samuel to consult, no harp to soothe, no vision to illumine, no priest to advise, and no God to answer his prayer; and in his despair, he resorted to a hag of a witch, and heard his doom pronounced once more in words than which none in the Bible are more poignant (I Samuel 18:15-19).

Sin is about Choices

The Bible teaches that sin is a matter of individual choice. It begins with discerning good from evil. Therefore, even when the choice to sin is made in the heart of the moment, the consequences remain. We made choices between right and wrong, good and evil, acceptable and unacceptable, pleasing and not pleasing, every day of our lives. These choices will determine our eternity.

I call heaven and earth to record this day against you, that I have set before you life and death, blessing and cursing; therefore, choose life, that both thou and thy seed may live (Deuteronomy 30:19).

And if it is unto you to serve the Lord, choose you this day whom ye will serve; whether the gods which your fathers served that were on the other side of the flood, or the gods of the Amorites, in whose land ye dwell; but as for me and my house we will serve the Lord (Joshua 24:15).

Saul is no more. He lies a corpse, with lonely Jonathan. How are the mighty fallen! How is this son of the morning brought to shame! Yes Saul- Saul of early promise, but of later decline and final ruin, you have "played the fool"! Oh, what warnings this man utters to us! God help us each to say, and really to mean it, "take my will, and make it thine; It shall be no longer mine. Take my intellect, and use every power as thou shalt choose! A foolish or bad choice can lead us into the spirit of deception. As Saul decays in characters, we shall see him deceiving himself and others more and more. His first deception at Gilgal occurred when he greeted Samuel cordially and expected the prophet to give him a blessing. Saul was playing the hypocrite and acting as though he had done nothing wrong. Your life is a result of the choices you make. If you don't like your life, it is time to start making better choices (Amy Poehler).

It was foolish of Saul to think that he could disobey God and get away with it, and that his disobedience could bring God's blessing on himself and his army. "Let us do evil that good may come" (Romans 3:8). Is the logic of hell, not the law of heaven. Saul was foolish to conclude that the sacrifice of a king at the wrong time was as good as the sacrifice of a priest at the right time. He was foolish to walk by sight and not by faith in God's promise.

"For whatsoever is not of faith is sin" (Romans 14:23). Saul had the same kind of superstitious faith that Eli's sons had when they carried the Ark on the battlefield. He knew nothing of the obedience of faith (Romans 16:26). Saul's pride, impatience, and deception were all seen and judged by the Lord, and Samuel, the prophet announced the sentence: The crown would eventually be taken from Saul and given to another, in this case, David. Despite some foolish and bad choices that Saul had made, he would continue as King, but he would not establish a lasting dynasty, and none of his sons would succeed him and rule over Israel. God wanted a king with a heart that was right toward God, a man with a shepherd's heart and he found that kind of heart in David (Acts 13:22). Our task isn't an enjoyable one as we watch the character of King Saul steadily deteriorate. He has already demonstrated his unbelief, impatience, and dishonesty. Saul's history will climax with the king visiting a witch and then committing suicide on the battlefield.

Sir Walter Scott made a poignant observation when he penned in his poem, Marmion, "What a tangled web we weave when first we practice to deceive!"

Chapter 10

The Magnitude of Choice

Sitting at the Gate of Sodom

Remember Lot. He had every advantage imaginable to know the Lord and to live his life to the fullest. He was taken in and reared by Abraham when Abraham first trusted God to begin his journey of faith. But he apparently paid little attention to the testimony and witness of Abraham (Genesis 12:4-5). He was given the first choice of land by Abraham, but chose selfishly and settled close to Sodom (Genesis 13:5-18). He was rescued from enslavement when captured by the invading army of Kings from the East (Genesis 14:12:16). But instead of returning with Abraham, he chose to return to Sodom.

Lot loved Sodom and the opportunities the city offered him for business and personal pleasure. Lot coveted the city's bright light, the opportunity for wealth, possessions, pleasure and opposition. Scripture gives a graphic picture of Lot's love for Sodom, the declining stages he went through in moving closer and closer to Sodom and its carnal and wicked way of life.

Lot first of all lifted up his eyes and looked upon Sodom and the rich, fertile valley of the Jordan in which the city sat (Genesis 13; 10-11). Lot then choose to move, pitching his tent toward Sodom (Genesis 13:12-13). Lot finally is seen sitting at the gate of Sodom, which meant that he was most likely some city official (Genesis 19:1). Lot began the pilgrimage to the Promised Land with Abraham. But once there, he saw the bright light and business opportunities of Sodom. Instead of focusing on the heavenly city, the promised land, he looked and looked at Sodom until the attraction of the city consumed him. Eventually, Lot became one with the city and its ungodly people.

Lot's life is a graphic picture of backsliding, a dangerous threat to us all. Lot was saved, genuinely saved. Scriptures say so.

"And God delivered just Lot, vexed with the filthy conversation of the wicked earth: for that righteous man dwelling among them, in seeing and hearing, vexed his righteous soul from day to day with their unlawful deeds" (2 Peter 2:7-8). But Lot fell back, lived a carnal, fleshly life. He was right at home with the sinful and wicked of the earth. What a perfect picture Lot exhibits of a modern-day carnal Christian! Lot was walking in the counsel of the ungodly, standing in the way of sinners, and sitting in the seat of the scornful (Psalm 1:1). Lot believed he had the best of both worlds, the eternal benefits of knowing the Lord as Savior, but also all the temporal benefits that result from worldly influence and possessions, together with acceptance by and fellowship with men of the world. Our lives are filled with choices. Some of our choices can be very simple, such as what we utter from our mouth, places we go, and the things we do. Other decisions are far more complicated. Our career, family, finances, morals of these areas certainly require tough decisions to be made. Therefore, choices whether good or bad, all have consequences. Let us reflect on the flood of Noah's time, the decisions made by Samson, the cause of the destruction of Sodom and Gomorrah, the choices of BELSHAZAR and NEBUCHADNEZZAR- these punishments all were the consequences of poor decision-making.

Choices made whether bad or good, follow you forever and affect everyone in their path one way or the other (J.E.B. Spredemann).

Listen to your heart. Listen to your instincts. Listen to your inner voice. It is your true self. It will guide you to make the right choices (Lailah G. Akita). Lot lifted up his eyes to "behold all the plain of Jordan, that it was well-watered everywhere, like the garden of the Lord" (Genesis 13:10). He did not ask what God had chosen for him. He did not consider the prejudicial effect which the morals of the place might exert upon his children and himself. His choice was entirely determined by the lust of the flesh, the lust of the eyes, and the pride of life. For the men of Sodom were "sinners before the Lord exceedingly."

Of course, if God sends a man to Sodom, He will keep him there; as Daniel was kept in Babylon: and nothing shall by any means hurt him. "He shall be kept as the eye is kept: guarded in his bony socket from violence, and by its delicate veil of eyelid sheltered from the dust." (F.B. Meyer). But if God does not clearly send a man to Sodom, it is a blunder, crime, a peril to go. Mark the fact that Lot was swiftly swept into the vortex. First he saw; then he chose; next, he journeyed east. After which, he pitched his tent toward Sodom, dwelt there, and finally, after becoming a magistrate or judge of the city, sat in the gate. His daughters married two of the men of Sodom, and they probably rank among the most prestigious and influential families of the neighborhood. But his power of witness-bearing was gone. Perhaps if he lifted up his voice in protest against deeds of shameless vice, he was laughed at for his stance, or threatened with violence. His righteous soul might become vexed, but was met with no sympathy. His property was destroyed during the annihilation of the cities. His wife was turned into a pillar of salt. And the blight of Sodom left a distinctive brand upon his daughters. Wretched, indeed, must have been the last days of that hapless man. Cowering in a cave, stripped of everything, face-to-face with the results of his shameful sin is, indeed, a terrible picture. Retribution is in store for everyone whose choice of home, friends, and surroundings, is dictated by the lust of worldly gain, fashion, or pleasure, rather than the will of God. If such are saved at all, they will be saved as Lot was - so as by fire.

The Choices We Make Will Dictate Our Destiny

Lot's final days were full of darkness and sin as he committed incest in a cave. He forsook a tent for a house in the city, ended up in a cave, and was made drunk by his daughters! Lot chose the wrong place and ruined himself and his loved ones. Abraham was visited in the day time but Lot in the evening. Abraham was at the tent door; Lot at the city gate. Abraham had power with God, but Lot had no influence even with his family. Abraham witnessed the destruction of Sodom, yet lost nothing, but Lot lost everything. Lot is remembered in a negative light, but the story of Abraham continues in a historically positive tone. As for Lot, the sun is no more needed for the day; nor the moon for the night. Lot was warned and finally heeded the word of God.

Because the Lord has become the everlasting light of the surrendered and separated heart, and the days of its mourning have passed away forever. For this cause, the Lord called Lot and his family to "come out from among them, and be ye separate, saith the Lord, and touch not the unclean thing and I will receive you, and be a father unto you; and ye shall be my sons and daughters, saith the Lord Almighty. Having, therefore, these promises, dearly beloved, let us cleanse ourselves from all filthiness of the flesh and spirit" (2 Corinthians 6:7).

How great was the contrast between Lot and Abraham? Lot lifted up his eyes, at the dictate of worthy prudence, to spy out his advantage. Abraham lifted up his eyes, not to discern what would best for his material interests, but to behold what God had prepared for him. How much better it is to keep our eyes steadfastly fastened upon the Lord till He says to us, "Lift up now thine eyes, and look from the place where though art - Northward, and Southward, and Eastward, and Westward: For all the land which thou seest, to thee will give it, and to thy seed forever" (Genesis 13:14-15). Lot had lived a hypocritical life: he had sat at the gate, judging and reproving the citizens of Sodom for their injustices while living a compromising and worldly life (see 2 Peter 2:8). The sign of backsliding is Lot's desire to linger in the world. This is a detailed picture of how far a believer can backslide. A believer can fall in love with the world despite the severe warnings of impending judgment. There was the urgent warning (verse 15). The two angels warned Lot: he needed to hurry, take his wife and two daughters and get out; flee the city lest they all be consumed. Lot lingered. But God had mercy on him: the two angels grabbed the hands of Lot, his wife, and daughters leading them out of the city. Despite his having just been saved from a catastrophic death by the great mercy of God. Despite his impending facing judgment, when the angels led Lot and his family outside the city, the angels had to warn Lot again and urged him to escape for his life, to flee to the mountains out of the plain lest he is consumed (verse 17). But Lot pleaded against God's will.

Thousands of years later we read of the warning and judgment of Sodom and Gomorrah, yet for generations, conduct similar behaviors. No wonder Jesus Christ said, "Verily I say unto you it shall be more tolerable for the land of land of Sodom and Gomorrah on the day of Judgment, than for that city" (Matthew 10:15).

"But the same day that Lot went out of Sodom it rained fire and brimstone from heaven and destroyed them all. Even thus shall it be in the day when the Son of man I revealed (Luke 17:29-30). "And turning the cities of Sodom and Gomorrah into ashes condemned them with an overthrown, making them an example unto those that after should live ungodly" (2 Peter 2:6). "Even as Sodom and Gomorrah, and the cities about them in like manner, giving themselves over to fornication, and going after strange flesh, are set forth, for example, suffering the vengeance of eternal fire (Jude 7).

The Lord Himself, however, gave great hopes to the Sodomites, the homosexuals of this earth. He said, that Sodom was judged and destroyed because of sin, but that it would not have been destroyed if its people had repented. "The backslider in heart shall be filled with his ways: and a good man shall be satisfied from himself" (Proverbs 14:14). And because iniquity shall abound, the love of many shall wax cold." (Matthew 24:12), after that, ye have known God, or rather are known of God, how turn ye again to the weak and beggarly elements, whereunto ye desire again to be in bondage? (Galatians 4:9). "For Demas hath forsaken me, having loved this present world" (2 Timothy 4:10). Now the just shall live by faith: but if any man draws back, my soul shall have no pleasure in him" (Hebrews 10:38).

"For if after they have escaped the pollutions of the world through the knowledge of the Lord and Saviour Jesus Christ, they are again entangled therein, and overcome, the latter end is worse with them than the beginning. For it had been better for them not to have known the way of righteousness, than, after they have known it, to turn from the holy commandment delivered unto them." (2Peter 2: 20-21). Because Lot followed the leading of angels and left the city, he escaped hearing the Lord say "Nevertheless I have somewhat against thee, because thou hast left thy first love" (Revelation 2:4)

"Your life is the sum result of all the choices you make, both consciously and unconsciously. If you can control the process of choosing, you can take control of all aspects of your life. You can find the freedom that comes from being in charge of yourself" (Robert F. Bennett).

Lot's covetous choice was the beginning of sorrows; the land posted a tempting posture, but with depraved neighbors. The men of Sodom were wicked before the Lord, and the outcome of Lot's choice is a sad chapter of sorrow and degradation for all of Lot's household (Genesis 19). How often God's people make the tragic mistake of pitching their tent too near to Sodom. Too near the borderline of separation- exposing their household to the contagious influence of a wicked world.

Although Lot became a well-known figure in Sodom, the price he paid for his poor decision was high because of the wickedness of Sodom and Gomorrah. God decided to destroy them. Abraham made intercessory prayer for these cities, but God's mind could not be changed. Not even ten righteous people could be found among them. All the inhabitants of Sodom and Gomorrah. Though God sent special angels to warn Lot and his family, their hearts was so entrenched in the city that it was hard for them to leave. His sons-in-law refused to leave, making fun of the warning. Hundreds of years later, Jesus recalled this incident to His disciples by saying, "Remember Lot's wife" (Luke 17:32). The message was simple and plain. He was telling them not to look back to the world of sin that they had left behind! "Be sure that life is made up of choices, and knowing to the fact that life is just a series of decisions we make, and depending on our choice, we must live with the result of that decision. When making a choice, one must be aware of its future ramifications in our lives. One should always remember that life is a series of choices; therefore, make a choice in your life during your earthly mission. Just think: The choice you make today could make not only your life happier, but make a better world in which we live." (James Van Prana).

Lot had a tent but no altar (Genesis 13:5); Which meant he did not call on the Lord for wisdom in making decisions. Instead of lifting up his eyes to heaven, Lot lifted up his eyes to the plain of Jordan (Genesis 13:10). The eyes see what the heart loves. Abraham had taken Lot out of Egypt, but he could not take Egypt out of Lot. Outlook helps to determine an outcome. Abraham's eyes were on the holy city of God (Hebrews 11:13-16), and he continued to walk with God and inherit blessings. Lot's eyes were on the sinful cities of men, and he went on to worldly success, spiritual failure, and a shameful end.

Lot had a great opportunity to become a man of God as he walked with Abraham, but we don't read that Lot built an altar or called on the Lord. First, Lot looked toward Sodom (Genesis 13:10); then he moved toward Sodom (13:11-12); and finally, he moved into Sodom (14:12). Instead of being a pilgrim who made progress, Lot regressed into the world and away from God's blessing (Psalm 1:1). He "journeyed east" (Genesis 13:11) and turned his back on Bethel ("House of God") and towards Ai "Ruins" (Genesis 12:8).

"The choices you make now, the people you surround yourselves with, they all have the potential to affect your life, even who you are, forever." (Sarah Dessen).

Chapter 11

The Brevity of Time

Time: A valuable element of life. Time is the elusive value that governs, dominates and limits man's very existence. You don't have to be a philosopher or a scientist to know that "Time and Seasons" are a standard part of life, no matter where you live. Were it not for the dependability of God-ordained "Natural laws" both science and daily would be chaotic, if not impossible. Not only are there times and seasons in this world, but there is also an overruling providence in our lives. Therefore, from before our birth to the moment of our death, God is accomplishing His divine purpose, even though we always don't understand He is doing. Today in a modern world racing towards tomorrow, and tomorrow. Time is a constant challenge. No matter how old you are, you have never lived this day. This day is a new piece of road. Each morning puts a man on trial and each evening passes judgment.

Mind and Spirit Do Not Grow Old

The Bible says, "And this is life eternal, that they might know thee the only true God" (John 17:3). The man who thinks or believes that the natural cycle of birth, adolescence, youth, maturity, and age is all there is to life, is indeed to be pitied. Such a man has no anchor, hope, nor vision; and to him, life has no meaning. If you cannot play a fast game of tennis, or swim as fast as a younger person, or if your body has slowed down, or you walk with a slow step, remember life is always clothing itself anew.

Ralph Waldo Emerson, poet, and philosopher, said, "We do not count a man's years until he has nothing else to count." Your character, the quality of your mind, your faith, and your convictions are not subject to decay.

The Cycle of Life Under the Sun

One of the marvelous mysteries of the universe is time. Like an incessant caravan, it moves on and past the great milepost of history, and on into eternity. It moves eternally with God and is indefinable. Time plays no favorites. It levels up. It bestows its favors impartially; 60 seconds to the minute, 60 minutes to the hour, 8760 hours to the year. Each man, whether poor or wealthy, young or old, great or unknown shares equally in the allocation of time.

His twenty-four day is no shorter or longer than that of his fellow man. This time is his to spend, second by second, hour by hour, day by day, year by year, as he alone chooses. It is his to spend wisely or foolishly, in daydreams or productivity, hate or love, fear or happiness, selfishness or contribution. The secret to peace with God is to discover, accept, and appreciate God's perfect timing. The danger is to doubt or resent God timing. This can lead to despair, rebellion, or move ahead without His advice. It is our responsibility to accept and cooperate with God's timing. Our alignment with God's timing makes a great difference. God has made everything appropriate in its time. God has put eternity in our hearts, so we must trust him to communicate His timing.

Live A Day At A Time

Too many people spend half of their lives living in the future. They dissipate their time, their energy, their thoughts, reacting to a situation which probably will never occur. This "dream world" saps their creativity. Life is simply a succession of a small union called days.

With a limited amount of time, we can't be or do everything we want to do. A person is always faced with a decision as to whom or what he wants to give his time. Remember everything takes time and our choices determine our destiny. This is one of the key points for an abundant dynamic living. Most of us spend fifty minutes an hour living in the past with regrets for lost joy, or shame for things badly done, or in a future which we either long for or dread.

Man's days are numbered. "The days of our years are threescore years and ten; and if by reason of strength they be fourscore years, yet is their strength labor and sorrow; for it is soon cut off, and we fly away so teach us to number our days

The Brevity of Time

That we may apply our hearts into wisdom (Psalm 90:10,12). For a human time, here on earth, the calculation is like this: Internal beats per minute 72; per hour 4,320; per day 103,650,838, 400. Total lifetime of 70 years is about 2.5 billion heartbeats. Time is the only sure test of anything. It is only the severest critic of all; it is the only true critic. You cannot judge the value of this or that on the spur of the moment, for only time can determine that will honor you for what you are. The year of the man's birth is marked in the calendar fails to tell us how many years a man has truly lived. One lives regarding desire and passion, joy and sorrow, vision and prayer. Time steals the strength from a man's muscle and the youthful beauty of a woman's face. Time robs us of our health and strips us at last of everything we have.

Dost thou love life? Then do no squander time, for that's the stuff life is made of (Benjamin Franklin).

Time is like a petal in the wind, flows softly by as old lives are taken, new ones begin a continual chain which lasts throughout eternity, every life but a minute in time but each of equal importance (Cindy Chenery, "Time") Life, death, time, and extremity: these are the ingredients that make up our brief experience in this world, and they must not be ignored. God has a time for everything, including judgment. He is working out His eternal purposes in and through the deeds of men, even the deeds of the wicked. Yes, God will judge when history has run its course.

The Apostle Paul addressed Timothy with these words: "For the time will come when they will not endure sound doctrine; but after their lusts shall they heap to themselves teachers, having itching ears (2 Timothy 4:3).

In this time that we are living, people will turn from the truth, they will grow weary of the plain gospel of Christ, they will be greedy for fables, and take pleasure in them. People do so when they do not endure that preaching which is searching, plain, and to the purpose.

"Truth that is naked is the most beautiful, and the simpler its expression the deeper is the impression it makes;

this is partly because it gets unobstructed hold of the hearer's mind without his being distracted by secondary thoughts, and partly because he feels that here he is not being corrupted or deceived by the arts of rhetoric, but that the whole effect is got from the thing itself." (Arthur Schopenhauer)

Let us seize the favorable opportunity for every useful purpose and live for God. The time to change our address is fast approaching, while labor and sorrow fill the world. This is given us that we may always have something to do; none were sent into the world to be idle. A time to be born, and a time to die; a time to plant and a time to pluck up that which is planted; a time to kill and a time to heal; a time to break down and a time to build up; a time to weep and a time to laugh; a time to mourn and a time to dance; A time to cast away stones, and a time to gather stones together; a time to embrace and a time to refrain from embracement; a time to get, and a time to cast away; a time to rend, and a time to sew; a time to love and a time to hate; a time of war; and a time of peace (Ecclesiastes 3:2-8).

Everything is as God made it; not as it appears to us. We have the world so much in our hearts, are so taken up with thoughts and cares of worldly things, that we have neither time nor spirit to see God's hand in them. The world has not only gained possession of the heart but has formed thoughts against the beauty of God's works. We mistake if we dare to think that we were born for ourselves. It is our business to do good in this life, which is short and uncertain; we have, but little time to be doing good, therefore we should redeem the time. Yea, the stork in the heaven knoweth her appointed times; and the turtle and the crane and the swallow observe the time of their coming; but my people know not the judgment of the Lord (Jeremiah 8:7). Time is in God's hand and not on our own, and we do not so much as know what we shall be on the morrow. "Go to now, ye that say today or tomorrow we will go into such a city, and continue there a year, and buy and sell, and get grain: Whereas ye know what shall be on the morrow. For what is your life? It is even a vapor that appeareth for a little time, and vanisheth away" (James 4:13-15).

To be familiar with the grave is prudence. To prepare for death, it is well to commune with death.

A thoughtful walk in the cemetery is good for our soul's health." (Charles Spurgeon). God's words tell us, "And it is appointed unto men once to die but after this the judgment." (Hebrews 9:27). We must find the guidelines we need in the observation of life and time, and the examination of our human nature. You can rest with this in your mind, "man shapes his to-morrow by his today. Finding purpose and fulfillment in life begins with understanding. God has added value and significance to our lives that He did not bestow on any of His other creatures. In Ecclesiastes 3, Solomon teaches us that God's ultimate plan for the human race rises above all the disappointments and dissatisfactions that are so common on earth. What makes people different, more valuable, than every other species? First human time and life differ from that of every other created being. And though every creature of God has its purpose, God added an important dimension to the life of man. Solomon explained it.

The Fact Stated: Everything has A Time And A Season

Solomon began this chapter by saying a very basic fact: "There is a time or season for everything, and also a time for every purpose or activity in man's life on earth (his days under heaven). Think about this statement for a moment; it is one that is often quoted, but Solomon fully understood. First, he was saying that man's life includes a variety of activities and experiences. Diversity and fluctuation mark our time on earth; it is not always the same, unchanging, monotonous routine. Second, the teacher emphasizing that the variety of events and experience in life are ordered and appointed by God. The specific words that the author uses in this verse are essential to understanding this great truth. In simple terms, a person's life is a variety of experiences, activities, and events controlled by God. Solomon is stressing the point that God's plan for our lives includes ups and downs, mountains and valleys, pleasure and pain. In His infinite wisdom, God knows we need to face problems and trials that will stir us to pray and draw closer to Him. Through such trials, we grow stronger and learn to trust Him more and more. Therefore, both good experiences and trials are needed for God to complete His purposes for us.

Within the appointed times and seasons, these colorful, thought-provoking pairs paint a collective portrait of the experience of life here on earth, according to Ecclesiastes 3.

1). Birth and death: There is an appointed time for every person in birth and a time for every person's death. God is the giver of life.

2). Planting and plucking the yearly cycle of climate declares that we do not sow and reap on our schedule but God's. We plant in the spring and harvest or uproot what we planted in the fall. It is God's cycle, and He has appointed seasons for both in our lives.

3). Killing (executing justice) and healing: When a person deliberately commits a murder, time is set for the execution of Justice.

4). Tearing down and building up: from the planning stages of a new building to the grand opening, the progression is an exciting experience. Nevertheless, a time comes when nearly all buildings age and deteriorate to the point that they must be demolished. Great structures like everything else, have a life cycle. This is another example of God's process of life.

5). Crying and laughing: these two extremes of human emotions remind us that life is filled with both tears and laughter, both sad and happy affairs, Joy and sorrow, celebrations and solemn assemblies, weddings and funeral these are all part of the fabrics of life.

6). What we laugh at and what we weep over indicates our values of life, and values are part of maturity. These six contrasts illustrate that God's plan for our lives involves a collection of diverse experiences. Opposite extremes in life- and everything in between- are controlled by the one who designs our days and years. The ultimate conclusion of all of Solomon's experimentation, study and research, the one invaluable, life-changing truth of Ecclesiastes, is this: "Fear God. Keep His commandments.

Chapter 12

Let Go and Let God

Life is a struggle. Life will throw curveballs at you, and humble you. It will attempt to break you down. And just when you think things are starting to look up, life will smack you back down with ruthless indifference. No matter how much we want things to stay the same, life is all about change. Sometimes change is for the better, and sometimes it's not. No matter why things are changing, we need to be able to let go and move on. Whether it's the death of a loved one, a painful breakup, a business failure, or a treacherous betrayal, holding on to past pain and resentment will only hold you back. (Davide Mancini)

Though we live wholly on mercy and forgiveness, we are hesitant to forgive the offenses of our brethren. In the book of Matthew 18:21-22, Peter came to Him and asked, "Lord, how many times will my brother sin against me and I forgive him and let it go? Up to seven times?" Jesus answered him, "I say to you, not up to seven times, but seventy times seven. "(Amplified Bible AMP)

This parable shows how much provocation God had from His family on earth, and how untoward His servants are. There are three ideas in the parable: (1) The Master's wonderful clemency. The debt of sin is so great that we are not able to pay it. See here what every sin deserves; this is the wages of sin, to be sold as a slave. It is the folly of many who are under strong convictions of their sin, to fancy they can make God satisfaction for the wrong they have done Him. (2) The servant's unreasonable severity toward his fellow-servant, notwithstanding his Lord's clemency toward him. (3) The Master reproved his servant's cruelty. The greatness of sin magnifies the riches of pardoning mercy, and the comforting sense of pardoning mercy does much to dispose of our hearts to forgive our brethren.

How justly will those be condemned, who, though they bear the Christian name, persist in a unmerciful treatment of their brethren! The humbled sinner relies only on free, abounding mercy, through the ransom of the death of Christ. Let us seek more and more for the renewing grace of God, to teach us to forgive others as we hope to receive forgiveness from Him. Peter doubtless thought that he was unusually liberal and generous in proposing such a measure of forgiveness. You see, seven is the number of completeness and plurality, and our Lord used it in giving His sentence about forgiveness:

"Forgiveness is not about forgetting. It is about letting go of another person's throat. Forgiveness does not create a relationship. Unless people speak the truth about what they have done and change their mind and behavior, a relationship of trust is not possible. When you forgive someone, you certainly release them from judgment, but without true change, no real relationship can be established. Forgiveness in no way requires that you trust the one you forgive. But should they finally confess and repent, you will discover a miracle in your own heart that allows you to reach out and begin to build a bridge of reconciliation between you. Forgiveness does not excuse anything. You may have to declare your forgiveness a hundred times the first day and the second day, but the third day will be less, and each day after, until one day you will realize that you have forgiven completely. And then one day you will pray for his wholeness......" (Paul Young)

How do we reach the goal that God has set for us? For one thing, we must be honest with ourselves and admit where we are, as Paul declared: "Not that I have already attained." Then, we must keep our eyes of faith on Christ our solid rock and forget the past sins and failures, and also past successes. We must press on in his power. You see, the Christian life is not a game; it is a race that demands the very best that is in us: The Apostle Paul says

"Brethren, I count not myself to have apprehended: but this one thing I do, forgetting those things which are behind, and reaching forth unto those things which are before, I press toward the mark for the prize of the high calling of God in Christ Jesus." (Philippians 3:13-14).

Too many Christians live divided lives. One part tries to live for the Lord. The other gets motivated by carnal desires and minding worldly ambitions. The Christian calling is a high and heavenly calling, and if we live for this world, we lose the prize that goes with the high calling.

Know ye not that they which run in a race run all, but one receiveth the prize? So run, that ye may obtain. And every man that striveth for the mastery is temperate in all things. Now they do it to obtain a corruptible crown, but we an incorruptible. I therefore so run, not as uncertainly; so fight I, not as one that beateth the air: But I keep under my body, and bring it into subjection: lest that by any means, when I have preached to others, I myself should be a castaway (1 Corinthians 9:24-27).

"But we have this treasure in earthen vessels, that the excellency of the power may be of God, and not of us. We are troubled on every side, yet not distressed; we are perplexed, but not in despair;" (2 Corinthians 4:7-8). "Ye did run well; who did hinder you that ye should not obey the truth?" (Galatians 5:7).

"Wherefore seeing we also are compassed about with so great a cloud of witnesses, let us lay aside every weight and the sin which doth so easily beset us, and let us run with patience the race that is set before us," (Hebrews 12:1).

Paul worked at forgetting his past. This is a verse that is of enormous help to believers who have failed God, miserably failed Him. Paul had so failed God, and he was always confessing that he fell far short He says, "For I know that in me (that is, in my flesh,) dwelleth no good thing: for to will is present with me; but how to perform that which is good I find not. For the good that I would I do not: but the evil which I would not, that I do "(Romans 7: 18-19).

Paul faced what so many of us face: failure and shortcoming, the struggle to forget it and to move on. How does a person do this? It is one of the most difficult things in all the world to do.

And it is especially difficult if others are not forgiving and willing to let the believer put his failure behind him. See how Paul tells us how to deal with the past? By concentrating and controlling the mind and by reaching forth to those things which are before us. Not the concentration and focus (a) "But one thing" (b) But this one thing I do. In one focused act, we must forget the things that are past and reach forth to those things that are before us. This act involves two parts: both forgetting and reaching forth. The past cannot be forgotten without reaching forth to what lies ahead. A person cannot sit around moaning and regretting the past. To do so is to be concentrating upon the past. The things of the past are to be the focus of the mind. The children of God must zero in on the things at hand and on the things that lie ahead. If we do this, there is no time to wallow in the past and its failure.

"Strive to enter in at the strait gate: for many, I say unto you, will seek to enter in, and shall not be able" (Luke 13:24).

"Therefore, my beloved brethren, be ye steadfast, unmovable, always abounding in the work of the Lord, forasmuch as ye know that your labor is not in vain in the Lord,"
(1 Corinthians 15:58).

"And let us not be weary in well doing: for in due season we shall reap, if we faint not," (Galatians 6:9).

"Behold, I come quickly: hold that fast which thou hast, that no man take thy crown," (Revelation 3:11).

We are accustomed to saying "Past, present and future" but we should view time as flowing from the future, into the present and then into the past. At least, the believer should be future oriented, "Forgetting those things which are behind". To forget, in the Bible means no longer to be influenced or affected. God promises "Their sins and iniquities will I remember no more" (Hebrews 10:17).

The Lord is not suggesting that He will conveniently have a bad memory! This is impossible with God. What the Lord is saying is, "I will no longer hold your sins against you. Your sins can no longer affect their standing with me nor influence my attitude toward them," so forgetting those things which behind suggest an impossible feat of mental and psychological gymnastics by which we try to erase the sins and mistakes of the past. It simply means that we break the power of the past by living for the future. Certainly, we cannot change the past, but we can alter the meaning of the past.

There were things in Paul's past that could have been weighted to hold him back, but they became inspirations to speed him ahead. The events did not change, but his understanding of them changed.

Let me share an excellent example with my precious readers: When Joseph met his brothers the second time and revealed himself to them, he held no grudge against them. To be sure, they had mistreated him, but he saw the past from God's point of view. As a result, he was unable to feel animosity toward his brothers. Joseph knew that God had a plan for his life - a race for him to run- and in fulfilling that plan and looking ahead, he embraced the power of the past. Regrets of the past shackle too many people. They are trying to run in the race by looking backward! No wonder they stumble and fall and get in the way of other folks! Some runners are being distracted by the successes of the past, not the failures you see, the things which are behind must be set aside in the things which are before must take their place. Jesus said, "without me, you can do nothing (see John 15: 5) God works in us that he might work through us. As we apply ourselves to the things of the spiritual life, God can mature us and strengthen us for the race. Please allow me to take another look at Peter's concern: Forgiveness- Relationship- Brotherhood -Unity- Seventy times seven is four hundred and ninety; but this is not the point Jesus is making. The question is how often we should forgive a brother? Peter answers till seven times? Jesus: "No, until seventy times seven, times seventy times seven and on and on through eternity. Forgiveness is a matter of the heart, not the mind. The mind will only keep a record of wrongs. A spirit of forgiveness does not measure and limit the number of times it will forgive.

A spirit of forgiveness will tolerate being wronged and hurt time after time, Why? There are several reasons why. Forgiveness knows no limits, no measure, no numbers of times that it will forgive. Forgiveness is a quality of the spirit. All spiritual things, substances, and realities such as love, mercy, grace, joy. Forgiveness cannot be measured or limited. Forgiveness is by its very nature spiritual and not physical. Therefore, forgiveness is without measure or limit, so it is to be known and practiced at every opportunity. Forgiveness is a quality and a reality of the spirit, therefore is to be a spirit of life. The spirit of forgiveness is to forgive seventy times seven. Good human relationships are impossible without a forgiving spirit. You see, offending others is common to all. We are all sinful, and we all offend much too often. No one walks perfectly or anywhere close to the way we should. If we kept score, there would be little time to do anything else. To keep relationships healthy, we need to know at least four things: (1) Coming short and sinning (2) failing and offending are common to us all (3) we all offended by failing. Ask yourself this question: Is it right or wrong to let go and let God? Harboring an unforgiving spirit makes that person ill-natured, self-centered, and spiritually immature. Unforgiveness means that a person has not grown to be like Christ in his nature of understanding. Compassion and love, peace and good health can be preserved only through a forgiving spirit. An unforgiving spirit causes as much disturbance and division as the offender. A person with an unforgiving spirit has stooped to the level of the offender and had, become an offender. Think: as long as you embrace an unforgiving spirit, there can never be peace. Disturbance, conflict, and division prevail. An unforgiving spirit also affects a person's emotions, mind, and body. It is the lack of peace, the lack of a good relationship with God and man that disturbs the normal functioning of the body mind and emotions. Ulcers, high blood pressure, disturbed thoughts and emotions and on and on- are the result of an unforgiving spirit. Let's consider the fact that we are all lead to see our huge debt of sin and service that we owe to our great God. To sin is to mismanage that life and to cause loss; therefore, sin puts us in debt to God. The debt is insurmountable and infinite. Sin bankrupts man and puts him in debt to God. We are so bankrupt by sin that nothing can ever pay our debt. Neither silver and gold nor any amount of wealth can pay our debt. "They trust in their wealth and boast themselves in the multitude of their riches; none of them can by any means redeem his brother, nor give to God a ransom for him" (Psalm 49:6-7)

Not by works of righteousness which we have done, but according to his mercy he saved us, by the washing of regeneration, and renewing of the Holy Ghost; which he shed on us abundantly through Jesus Christ our Saviour; (Titus 3:5-6). For if ye forgive men their trespasses, your heavenly Father will also forgive you (Matthew 6:14) In whom we have redemption through his blood, the forgiveness of sins, according to the riches of his grace; (Ephesians 1:7). If we confess our sins, He is faithful and just to forgive us our sins, and to cleanse us from all unrighteousness. (1 John 1:9). The needle-eye prophet Isaiah tells us, "I, even I am he that blotteth out thy transgressions for mine own sake, and will not remember thy sins (Isaiah 43:25 KJV) I have blotted out, as a thick cloud, thy transgressions, and, as a cloud, thy sins: return unto me; for I have redeemed thee (Isaiah 44:22).

You see, the believer is living a life of righteousness and purity, honesty and truthfulness. The world often opposes such behavior. Therefore, the worldly person often opposes and abuses the believer. The believer is bearing testimony of the corruption of the world and to God's salvation. Man's need to escape the corruption by turning to Jesus Christ and His righteous. The point is this: the believer is not to react to a person who mistreats and does evil against him.

Two reasons why you shouldn't "Let go and let God" (1) Negative reaction will most likely cause the loss of friendship of the person and dashed the hope of ever reaching the person for Christ. On the other hand, if the believer returns good for evil, he opens the door for eventual friendships and bears testimony to the love of God for all men, even for those who do evil. (2) The negative reaction is not the way of God and Christ. The believer is to bless those who do evil against him. The word blesses mean to speak well to our persecutors. We do not react to them by cursing, speaking harshly or striking out at them. We do not try to hurt them either verbally or physically.

Chapter 13

Be Thankful

"**O**h that men would praise the Lord for his goodness, and for his wonderful works to the children of men" (Psalm 107:8) By him therefore let us offer the sacrifice of praise to God continually that is, the fruit of our lips giving thanks to His name (Hebrews 13:15).

This is the will of God that you should be thankful always. "Give thanks always, for you recognize the duty of doing God's will." "Give thanks always, for God has no wish to give you cause for sorrow: His will towards you is to fill you with thankfulness." We are to rejoice in creature comforts as if we rejoice not, and must not expect to live many years, and rejoice in them all; but if we do rejoice in God, we may do that evermore. A truly religious life is a life of constant joy. We shall see cause to give thanks for sparing and preventing, for common and uncommon, past and present temporal and spiritual mercies. Not only for prosperous and blessing, but also for afflicting providences, chastisements and corrections. In everything give thanks. "Giving thanks always for all things unto God and the Father in the name of our Lord Jesus Christ" (Ephesians 5:20)

"Rejoice… and be glad also with exceeding joy- happy are ye." The world cannot understand how difficult circumstances can produce exceeding joy because the world has never experienced the grace of God. Peter name several privileges that we share that encourage us to rejoice in the midst of fiery trials. It is an honor and a privilege to suffer with Christ and be treated by the world the way it treated Him. The fellowship of his suffering is a gift from God. Not every believer grows to the point where God can trust him with this kind of experience, so we ought to rejoice when the privilege comes to us.

"And they (the Apostles) departed from the presence of the Council, rejoicing that they were counted worthy to suffer shame for his name,"

(Acts 5:41). Christ is with us in the furnace of persecution. When the three Hebrew children were cast into the fiery furnace, they discovered that they were not alone (Daniel 3:23-25). The Lord was with Paul in all of his trials (Acts 23:11, 27:21-25) and He promises to be with us to the end of the age. Our suffering means glory in the future. You see, the world believes that the absence of suffering means glory, but the Christian's outlook is different. The suffering and trial of our faith today is the assurance of glory when the Lord returns. "Mature people know that life includes some postponed pleasures." Count it all joy, my brethren, when ye fall into divers temptation; knowing this, that the trying of your faith worketh patience, but let patience have her perfect work, that ye may be perfect and entire, wanting nothing. Let us take a look at David the king when he changed his behavior before Abimelech who drove him away, and he departed. He said, "I will bless the Lord at all times: His praise shall continually be in my mouth. My soul shall make her boast in the Lord; the humble shall hear thereof and be glad. O magnify the Lord with me and let us exalt His name together" (Psalm34:1-3).

I will bless the Lord at all times; even in the times of adversity. If the statement in the title may be relied upon, David's fortunes were now at the lowest ebb. He had fled from the court of Saul upon finding that Saul was determined to put him to death (1 Samuel 20:31). He had hoped to find a safe refuge with Achish but had been disappointed. He was at the point of becoming a fugitive and an outlaw a dweller in dens and caves of the earth (1 Samuel 22:1.) He had as yet no body of followers. We cannot help but admire his piety in composing a song of thanksgiving to God when declaring, "His praise shall continually be in my mouth." The word continually must be understood as meaning either every day or many times every day, but must not be taken quite literally, or the business of life would be at a standstill (Gill's Exposition of the Bible). I will bless the Lord at all times. This implies to ascribe blessings giving honor, praise, and glory to Him, for every temporal mercy. Every day and at all times in the day. Since these are renewed every morning, and continue all the day long: and as the God of grace for all spiritual blessings;

and that continually, because of these last always. Saints have reason to bless God in times of adversity as well as prosperity. Since it might have been worse with them than it is; they have a mixture of mercy in all. And all things work together for their good, and His praise shall continually be in my mouth. Not the praise of which God is the author, but of which he is the object, which is due him. This praise is due Him because of the perfection of his nature, and the works of his hands and the blessings of his providence and grace. This, the psalmist says should be in his mouth. His meaning is that he should not only retain in his heart a grateful sense of the divine favors but should express it with his lips. Should both make melody in his heart to the Lord and vocally sing his praises; and that continually, "as long as he lived, or had any being" (Psalm 146:2). Bless the Lord, O my soul…His better part, his soul which comes immediately from God and returns to Him, which is immaterial and immortal, as of more worth than the world. God is to be served with the best we have, the best of our substance. So with the best of our persons and it is the heart or soul, which requires being given Him. Such service as is performed with the soul or spirit is most agreeable to him. "Bless the Lord; not by invoking or conferring a blessing on Him, which as it is impossible to be done. So, He stands in no need of it. Believing God, all sufficient, and blessed for evermore; but by proclaiming and congratulating His blessedness, and by giving him thanks for all mercies, spiritual and temporal. And utilizing all that is within me bless His holy name; meaning not only all within his body, his heart reigns, but all within his soul, all the powers and faculties of it, his understanding, will, affections and judgment; and all the grace that was wrought him. Faith, hope, love, joy and the like, he will have all concerned and employed in praising the name of the Lord. Our Lord is exalted above all blessing and praise is great and glorious in all the earth by reason of his works wrought and blessings of goodness bestowed and which appears to be holy in them all as it does in the works of creation, providence and redemption; at the remembrance of which holiness and thanksgiving should be given for He that is glorious in holiness. (Psalm 97:12).

Our God, the great Creator, is worthy to be praised by us for that highest style of adoration which is intended by the term bless.

"All thy works praise thee O God, but thy saints shall bless thee." Our very life and essential self should be engrossed with this delightful service, and each one of us should arouse his own heart to the engagement. Therefore, let others forbear if they can: Bless the Lord O, my soul. Let others murmur.

But do thou bless? Let others bless themselves and the idols, but do thou bless the Lord. Let others use only their tongues, but as for me I will cry, "Bless the Lord O my soul and all that is within me bless his holy name." Many are our faculties, emotions, and capacities, but God has given them all to us all to join in chorus to his praise. Half-hearted, ill-conceived, unintelligent praises are not such as we should render our loving God. If the law of justice demanded all our heart, soul and mind for the creator, much more might violate the law of gratitude put in a general claim for the homage of our whole being to the God of grace. It is instructive to note that the Psalmist dwells upon the holy name of God as if his Holiness were dearest to him. Perhaps because the holiness or wholeness of God was in his mind the grandest motive for rendering to him the homage of his nature in its wholeness. "Bless the Lord O my soul" means he is consumed with the intensity to pay tribute, so, again calls upon himself to arise. Had he been very sleepy before? Or was he now doubly sensible of the importance; The imperative necessity of adoration? Indeed, he uses no vain repetitions for thus he shows that we have the need, again and again, to be still ourselves when we are about to praise our God. For it would be shameful to offer him anything less than the most our souls can render.

Remember when the Persian king could not sleep, so he read the Chronicles of the Empire and discovered that one who had saved his life had never been rewarded. How quickly did he bestow honor upon him? The Lord has saved us with a great salvation. Shall we render no recompense? The label ingrate is a shameful one that a man can wear. Surely, we cannot be content to run the risk of such a brand. Let us awake then and with intense enthusiasm bless our God, who forgiveth all thine iniquities: Here David begins his list of blessings received, which he rehearses as themes and arguments for praise. He selects a few of the choicest pearls from the casket of divine love, threads them on the string of memory and hangs them about the neck of gratitude, pardoned seen is, in our experience one of the choices boons of grace, one of the earliest gifts of mercy.

Be Thankful

"What shall I render unto the Lord for all his benefits toward me? I will take the cup of salvation and call upon the name of the Lord. I will pay my vows unto the Lord now in the presence of all his people. I will offer to thee the sacrifices of thanksgiving. I will call upon the name of the Lord (Psalm 116:12-14, 17).

What return can be equal to his bounties; what will be a proper acknowledgment of them; with what can I repay for them all the question is a natural and an appropriate question. It is one which we naturally ask when we have received a favor from our fellow mortals; how appropriate is it given the favor which we receive from God, especially because of the mercies of God! What can be an adequate return for love like that, for mercies so great so undeserved? Barnes notes; when we can praise God with our whole heart, we need to be willing for the entire world to witness our gratitude and joy in Him. And so, those who rely on his loving-kindness and truth through Jesus Christ will ever find him faithful to his word. If God gives us strength in our souls to bear the burdens, resist the temptations, and to do the duties of an afflicted state; If He strengthens us to keep hold of Himself by faith; And to wait with patience for the event, we are bound to be thankful. Paul and Silas have had their midnight hour "And at midnight Paul and Silas prayed, and sang praises unto God: and the prisoners heard them" (Acts16: 25).

The consolations of God to his suffering sons are neither few nor small. How much happier are true Christians than their prosperous enemies! As in the dark, so out of the depths, we may cry unto God. No place, no time is amiss, for praising God, if the heart is lifted up to Him. No trouble, however grievous should hinder us from praise. What a scene, the dark inner dungeon; the prisoners fast in the stocks, their backs still bleeding and smarting from the stripes; the companionship of criminals and outcasts of society; the midnight hour; not groans, nor curses, nor complaints, but joyous truthful songs of praise ringing through the vaulted walls? While their companions in the jail listened with astonishment to the heavenly sound in that place of shame and sorrow (Pulpit Commentary).

Paul and Silas were cheerful, notwithstanding the stripes that were laid upon them, and though their feet were made fast in the stocks, and they were in the innermost prison in a most deplorable and uncomfortable condition. And though they might be in expectation of greater punishment of and of death itself; but also, that they were thankful and glorified God, who had counted them worthy to suffer for His name's sake (Gill's Exposition of the Entire Bible),

There was the sharp witness of these two men, Paul and Silas. These men had just been stripped, beaten with rods, imprisoned and put in chains; their backs were a lacerated bloody swollen mess of human flesh. We can just imagine the excruciating pain. But note: sitting there in the dark, smelly, rat and roach infested dungeon, they bore a strong testimony is the wonderful grace of God. They praised and thanked God for his salvation, the privilege of suffering for the name of Christ Jesus. His presence and strength through all the suffering. All this took place at midnight, and they sang so loudly that the other prisoners could hear them. They were unashamed of the Lord. Be not thou, therefore, ashamed of the testimony of our Lord, nor of me his prisoner: but be thou partaker of the afflictions of the gospel according to the power of God; (2 Timothy 1-8).

The idea is that praying and singing went on throughout the night. The point to see is the strong testimony that bore through the terrible trial. For our light affliction, which is but for a moment worketh for us a far more exceeding and an eternal weight of glory (2 Corinthians 4:17). Praise, in its essence, is adoration of God. For a workable definition, however, we must qualify this. Praise is always active, assertive, demonstrative and open. It is not passive, presumptuous, undemonstrative nor secretive. Therefore, wherever praise is mentioned, movement, actions, sounds, and songs are seen and heard. The fatalist can never praise the Lord for the fatalist's underlying philosophy denies that life will come to any good and that ultimately any good can come to life. The pessimist can never sing the song of joy and praise. He simply does not have a supporting philosophy nor expectant perception.

For our perspective on praise, turn to Revelation 4. John was on the Isle of Patmos for the testimony of Jesus Christ (Revelation 1:9.

He had in his old age suffered the ultimate rejection of his society and was banished to this lonely place to live out the remaining days of his life. His surroundings offered no hope; his associates were the castaways of society. His friends were far away as if they were no longer alive, and memories haunted his mind as hundreds of friends who had been called upon to make the supreme sacrifice of their lives for the sake of the gospel. If ever a man had a reason to feel depressed and be entirely justified, it was John on Patmos. The church ever was being persecuted. It was unsafe to be a Christian and any part of the Roman Empire. The man who sat on the throne hated Christianity and Christians and seemed committed to wiping them off the face of the earth.

It is at this dark moment in the life of John that we come to the vantage point of praise. In Psalm 30:11-12, David says, "you turned my wailing into dancing, remembered my sackcloth and clothe me with joy, that my heart may sing to you and not be silent" Again the purpose of deliverance and salvation is to praise God. It does not depreciate nor does praise for the church. Praise is not only the symbol of excellence and blessing; it is our chief means of protection. The Hallelujah factor (Jack Taylor). We have now reached the last summit of the mountain chain of praise. It rises high into the clear azure, and its brow is bathed in the sunlight of the eternal world of worship. It is the rapture. The Psalmist David and Apostle Paul are full of inspiration and enthusiasm. They stay not to argue, to teach, nor to explain, but cry with burning words: "Praise Him. Praise, Him praise ye the Lord."

Chapter 14

The Moral and Social Life

The words of the preacher the son of David King in Jerusalem: "vanity of vanities said the preacher vanity of vanities all is vanity (Ecclesiastes 1:1-3).

We have various scenarios in our life. We invent, adopt, are led by, and measure ourselves against our personal narratives. These are usually commensurate with our personal histories, predilections, our abilities, limitations, and skills. We are not likely to invent a story which is wildly out of sync with ourselves. We rarely judge ourselves by a narrative which is not somehow correlated to what we can reasonably expect to achieve; In other words, we are not likely to frustrate and punish ourselves knowingly; Therefore, as we grow older, our narrative influx changes. Parts of it may be realized, which increases our self-confidence, sense of self-worth and self-esteem. It makes us feel fulfilled, satisfied and at peace with ourselves.

Vanity of vanities lamented Solomon "all is vanity" Solomon liked that word vanity. He used it thirty-eight times in Ecclesiastes as he wrote about "Life under the Sun." The word means emptiness, futility, vapor, that which vanishes quickly and it leaves nothing behind." From the human point of view ("Under the Sun"), life does not appear futile; and it is easy for us to get pessimistic. The Jewish writer Shalom Aleichem once described life as "A blister on top of a tumor and boil on top of that." You can almost feel that definition! The American poet Carl Sandburg compared life to "an onion, you can peel it off one layer at a time, and sometimes you weep, " and a British playwright George Bernard Shaw said that "life was a series of inspired follies."

You will find this important phrase twenty-nine times in Ecclesiastes and with it the phrase, "under the sun" under the heaven; it defines the outlook of the writer as he looks at life from a human perspective and not necessarily from heaven's point of view. He applies his wisdom and experience to the complexity of human situations and tries to make some sense out of life. As we now embark upon the sayings of Solomon, let us keep his viewpoint in mind: he is examining "life under the sun" in his unfolding message of God's Holy Word. G Campbell Morgan puts Solomon's outlook entirely in his words: "This man had been living through all these experiences under the sun, concerned with nothing above the sun until there came a moment in which he had seen the entirety of life." And there was something over the sun. It is only as a man who takes account of that which is under the sun that things under the sun are seen in the true light. The message is for the hour in which we live; after all, the society investigated a millennium before the birth of Christ was not too different from our world today. Solomon saw injustice to the poor (Ecclesiastes 4:1-3), crooked politics (5:8), materialism (5:10), a desire for good old days (7:10), guilty people allowed to commit more crime (8:11), and incompetent leaders (10:17).

If you have never trusted Jesus Christ as your savior, this I urge you to do and that without delay, why? Because no matter how much wealth, education or social prestige you may have, life without God is futile. The enjoyment of this world may temporarily satisfy that longing in your soul. You may search the wide world over, but you'll be just as before. You never find true satisfaction until you have found the Lord, for only Jesus can satisfy your soul. If you could have the fame and fortune, all the wealth you could attain, if you have not Christ within, your living here would be in vain. There'll come a time when death will find you. Riches cannot help you then. So, come to Jesus, only he can satisfy (Lanny Wolfe).

You are only chasing after the wind if you expect to find satisfaction own personal fulfillment in the things of this world. "For what shall it profit a man if he should gain the whole world and lose his soul?" Solomon experimented with life and discovered that there was no lasting satisfaction in possessions, pleasures, power, or prestige. He had everything yet his life was empty!

Everything Changes and Ends

The first given of life is that changes and endings are inevitable for any person, relationship, enthusiasm or thing. Nothing is perfect, permanently satisfying or permanently anything. Everything falls apart in time. Every beginning leads to a finale. Built in all experiences, persons, places and things is a lifespan. Our relationships pass through phases, from romance, through struggles to commitment. Then they end with death or separation. Here are some paradoxes we can joyously embrace as we recognize the true value of life.

Although everything changes and ends, things renew themselves and move through cycles that further our commitment. Although life is not always fair, something in us remains committed to fairness and refuses to be unjust or retaliate. Although suffering is part of life, we have ways of dealing with it, and thereby we expand our ability to handle pain and help others during their time of grief.

The paradox above shows the positive dimension in each of the conditions of existence; we advance in patience, forbearance, wisdom, appreciation, and perseverance. Life is not always fair, and neither are people. Sometimes we are maltreated. Sometimes we do all the right things and wind up losing. Sometimes we act cautiously and are nonetheless hurt. Others may be generous to us, and yet we take advantage of their kindness. Or we may act with good intentions toward others, and yet our efforts go unappreciated or misinterpreted. It may seem to us, that sometimes the divine asks too much of us: what we can bear is directly proportional to the inner strength and resources we have gathered in the course of life. Since life is a journey, we grow not only by a conquest of fear but also by occasional surrender to it. Therefore, the fact that we are given more than we can bear at times is not a flaw in our life or us but one of the ways we fulfill our cells by dismantling our ruggedly individualistic egos. No wonder Solomon cites the monotony of life as his first argument to prove that life is not worth living. All of this is true only if you look at life "under the sun" and leave God out of the picture. Then the world becomes a closed system that is uniform, predictable, unchangeable. It becomes the world where there are no answers to prayer and no miracles; for nothing can interrupt the cycle of nature.

If there is a God in this kind of world, He cannot act on our behalf because He is in prison and within the "Laws of Nature" that cannot be suspended. However, God does break into nature to do great and wonderful things! He does hear and answer prayer and works on behalf of his people. He held the sun in place so Joshua could finish a major battle (Joshua 10:6-14). He moved the sun assigned to King Hezekiah (Isaiah 38:1-8). He opened the Red Sea, and the Jordan River for Israel (Exodus 14; Joshua. 3:4). He turned off the rain for Elijah and then turned it on again (James 5:17-18). He calmed the wind and the waves for the disciples (Mark 4:35-41) and in the future, will use the forces of nature to bring terror and judgment to the people of the earth (Revelation 6). "There is but one step from the sublime to the ridiculous." Napoleon made this statement after his humiliation and retreat from Moscow in the winter of 1812. The combination of stubborn Russian resistance and a severe Russian winter was too much for the French army, and its expected victory was turned into shameful defeat. As part of his quest for "the good life" King Solomon examined everything from the life to the life to come. He said, "I turned myself to behold" simply means, "I considered things from another viewpoint." What he did was to look at his wisdom (Ecclesiastes 2:12-17) and his wealth (18-23) in light of the certainty of death. What good is it to be wise and wealthy if you're going to die and then leave everything behind? Solomon could not easily handle the subject as he looked at life "under the sun" for death is one of the obvious facts of life. The wise man sees that deficit coming and lives accordingly, while the fool walks in darkness and is caught unprepared.

The sinner may heap up all kinds of riches, but he can never truly enjoy them because he has left God out of his life. In fact, his riches may finally end up going to the righteous. This is not always the case, but God does make it happen that "the wealth of the sinner is laid up for the just" (Proverbs 13:22). Apart from God, there can be no true enjoyment of blessings or enrichment of life. It is good to have things that money can't buy. There was no reason to suppose that's a man's life has more meaning than the life of the humblest insect that crawls from one habitation to another (Joseph Wood Krutch). We are not like insects. Dr. Krutch knew that insects have life cycles, but men and women have histories. One bee is pretty much like another bee, but people are unique, and no two stories are the same.

First of all, Solomon saw something above men. A God who is in control of time and who balanced life's experiences. Then he saw something with a man that links him to God. Eternity in his heart. Thirdly, Solomon saw something ahead of man, the certainty of death. Finally, he saw something around a man, the problems and burdens of life under the sun (Ecclesiastes 4:1-5,13).

"Come now, all rich man, burst into loud weeping, wailing and crying aloud, because of your miseries which are coming up on you. Your wealth has rotted away, and your garments have become moth-eaten. Your gold and silver have become completely tarnished and corroded and their rust shall be for a witness against you and shall eat your flesh like fire. You stored up treasure in the last days. Behold, the pay of the laborers who mowed your fields which have been withheld by you cries out. And the cries of those who reap to have entered the ears of the Lord of Hosts. You spent a luxurious life upon the earth and lived voluptuously. You fattened your hearts in a day of slaughter. You condemned, you murdered the just and upright person, and he does not resist you." (The New Testament expanded translation, Kenneth S. Wuest). Go to now, is a call to anyone to consider his conduct as being wrong. How intelligent worldly and contriving men are to leave God out of their plans! How vain it is to look for anything good without God's blessing and guidance! The frailty, shortness, and uncertainty of life, ought to check the vanity and presumptuous confidence of all projects for futurity. We can fix the hour and minute of the sun's rising and setting to-morrow, but we cannot fix the certain time of vapor being scattered. So short, unreal, and fading is human life, and all the prosperity or enjoyment that attends it; though bliss or woe forever must be according to our conduct during this fleeting moment" (Matthew Henry's Commentary),

Solomon repeats his text. Vanity of vanities, all is vanity. These are the words of one that could speak by dear- bought experience of the vanity of the world which can do nothing to ease men of the burden of sin. As he considered the worth of souls, he gave good heed to what he spake and wrote; words of truth will always be an acceptable word.

And nails to such as are wandering and draw aside; means to establish the heart, that we may never sit loose to our duty, nor be taken from it (Matthew Henry's Commentary).

The clearest way to show what the rule of law means to us in everyday life is to recall what has happened when there is no rule of law. Today there is a great ideological struggle going on in the world. Outside upholds what it calls the materialistic dialectic. Denying the existence of spiritual values maintains that man responds only to worldly influences and consequently he is nothing. Now, on our side, we recognize right away that man is not merely an animal. His life and ambitions have at its core, a foundation of spiritual value. "In this life, there must be a willingness to take risks. Far better is it to dare mighty things, to win glorious triumphs, even though checkered by failure... than to rank with those poor spirits who neither enjoy nor suffer much, because they live in a gray twilight that knows not victory nor defeat," (Theodore Roosevelt). A positive self-concept, clear goals, hard work, and a willingness to take risks- all contribute to success. But there is a major obstacle to experiencing success and satisfaction in life.

Live purposefully to achieve your dreams and be the person you want to be; you must seek to have the right focus. Don't compare your life to other people's lives. For we have not the 'courage' to rank ourselves among or compare ourselves with, certain individuals distinguished by their self-commendation. They are not wise, measuring themselves, as they do, by one another and comparing themselves with one another. (2 Corinthians 10:12 Weymouth New Testament). Unfortunately, many people are living in and around our society who measure their success by comparing it to the success of those around them. It was David, King of Israel and Judah who saw the prosperity of the wicked. To the King the wicked were productive, profitable producing wealth and financially fruitful.

"Behold, these are ungodly, who prosper in the world; they increase in riches. Verily I have cleansed my heart in vain and washed my hands in innocency."

For all the day long have I been plagued, and chastened every morning. If I say, I will speak thus; behold, I should offend against the generation of thy children. When I thought to know this, it was too painful for me; until I went into the sanctuary of God; then understood I their end" (Psalm 73:12-17) take a moment to believe in yourself.

If you are going to be successful in creating the life of your goal and your dreams, you have to believe that you are capable of making it come to pass. In this life, there are many questions that we confront:

Nothing seems to change; The earth appears to abide forever, even as generations of men come and go; The sun is constant with its rising and setting; The winds continue their whirling cycle; Therefore, any effort to live without God can only be vanity as we find His purpose inexplicable.

I returned and saw under the sun that the race is not to the swift, nor the battle to the strong, neither yet bread to the wise, nor yet riches to men of understanding, nor yet favor to men of skill; but time and chance happeneth to them all (Ecclesiastes 9:11).

REFERENCES

(1) John Philips Commentary Series Exploring the Old Testament (Kregel Publication)

(2) The Bible Exposition Commentary Old Testament by Warren Wiersbe, (David C. Cook Publisher)

(3) Malley's Bible Handbook NIV (Zondervan Publication)

(4) The Matthew Henry Study Bible (Hendrickson Publishers)

(5) Explore the Book by J. Sidlow Baxter (Zondervan Publication)

(6) The Unfolding Drama of Redemption: W. Graham Scroggie (Kregel Publication)

(7) The Supreme Philosophy of Man -The Law of Life: Alfred Armand Montapert

(8) The Life of Joseph: F.B. Meyer - Christian Living Classics

(9) Strength for the Storm: Richard Exley

(10) The Preachers Outline and Sermon Commentaries (Volumes I and II)

(11) Distilled Wisdom: Alfred Armand Montapert